Rony O'Neill

WHIGS ON THE GREEN

Whigs on the Green

Edited by

CORNELIUS F. SMITH and BERNARD SHARE

GILL AND MACMILLAN

Published in Ireland by
Gill and Macmillan Ltd
Goldenbridge
Dublin 8
with associated companies in
Auckland, Delhi, Gaborone, Hamburg, Harare,
Hong Kong, Johannesburg, Kuala Lumpur, Lagos, London,
Manzini, Melbourne, Mexico City, Nairobi,
New York, Singapore, Tokyo
© The Editors and Contributors, 1990
0 7171 1820 7

Design by Jarlath Hayes
Print origination by
Seton Music Graphics Ltd, Bantry, Co. Cork
Printed by
Criterion Press, Dublin

Contents

Acknowledgments

The editors acknowledge with gratitude the assistance of many individuals and institutions. While it is impossible to record all who contributed with their knowledge and expertise they are particularly indebted to the following:

Individuals: Asher Benson, Basil Brindley (without whose infectious enthusiasm this book would scarcely have been possible), L.M. Cullen, Mairead Dunleavy, Donal Gillman, J.B. Lyons, R.B. McDowell, Kevin B. Nolan, Maurice R. O'Connell, Howard J. Robinson, Charles Chenevix Trench; and the families of deceased Members of the Stephen's Green Club.

Institutions: Allied Irish Banks, Bank of Ireland, British Library, Civic Museum, Dublin (Pat Johnston), Garda Museum, Gilbert Collection, Institute of Chartered Accountants of Ireland, Institution of Engineers of Ireland, Irish Architectural Archive, King's Inns, Linen Hall Library, Belfast, Masonic Order, National Archives, National Gallery of Ireland, National Library of Ireland (Messrs Kissane and O Luanaigh), National Museum of Ireland (Mairead Dunleavy), Quaker Library, Records Office at Dublin Castle, Royal Dublin Society, Royal Institute of Architects of Ireland, Royal Irish Academy, Stillorgan Public Library, Stock Exchange, Dublin, Trinity College Library, Turf Club, University College, Dublin Library.

The editors and publisher are grateful to the National Gallery of Ireland for permission to reproduce the illustrations on p. 157 and in the colour section; to Pat Liddy for the drawing on p. 37, from his book *Dublin Today*; and to Mrs. Caroline Murphy, and Eoin O'Brien for the illustration on p. 84 from the latter's *The Beckett Country*.

From among a wealth of personalities we have endeavoured to select a representative cross-section of biographies. Members who are still alive are not included, except *jure officii*. A date in brackets after a name indicates the year of election to Club Membership.

CFS
BS

Footprints . . . that perhaps another . . .

Introduction by BASIL BRINDLEY

Isn't it quite incredible to reflect that, as members and friends of members, we have been sailing o'er the very same threshold and up the grand old staircase of our beautiful home without interruption for the past hundred and fifty years?

In his wonderful architectural contribution to this Sesquicentennial History, Austin Dunphy describes the stucco work in the Dining Room, in the Reading Room and on the Staircase in minute detail and he leaves us in no doubt that 'we are custodians of works of art equal, in their way, to any in the world.'

He goes on to tell us that our staircase dates from about 1756 and that the beautiful scroll at the bottom is almost entirely carved from one piece of timber – 'Nowadays we could not even get the timber to make it, let alone the craftsmen to set it out and carve it.'

Is it any wonder, then, that so many of us are unashamedly proud of our close association with this magnificent Dublin house which Lord Killanin describes as 'part of our heritage'? His Lordship also expresses a nice touch of personal sentimentality in his 'Clubbable Man' when he relates that 'I am still very happy to be able to totter in and meet my many friends.'

Thankfully he may continue to totter in and out as often as he pleases now that the fortunes of the Club are showing such a very welcome recovery and earlier thoughts of relocation have finally been laid to rest.

To many of us the Stephen's Green Club is our Town House — a home from home in which we may entertain our companions or relax in the company of fellow members. It has been that way since the days of Daniel O'Connell and there is no reason why our liberal outlook and our traditional camaraderie shouldn't continue for many, many successive generations.

Preparation for the sesquicentennial celebrations commenced some three years ago and the Club History which you are about to read is the result of a combined effort on the part of very many members.

Two 'Schooling Hurdles' had to be cleared before we were able to enter the Historical Race itself. The first objective was to locate the missing minutes and the second to obtain substantial support from a suitable sponsor.

Pursuit of those elusive records had proved fruitless for longer than many successive committee members would care to admit. All outside sources had been exhausted and 1990 was almost upon us when a final last ditch decision was made to scour the house from top to bottom and, *Mirabile dictu*, it was the bottom that came up trumps. Right down in the basement on Tuesday, 1st August 1989 to be precise.

Flushed with success after clearing that first hurdle, the second was taken in full flight and, thanks to some friendly co-operation Allied Irish Banks made sure that *Whigs on the Green* would be a confirmed runner in the 'Sesquicentennial Stakes'.

At this stage particular mention must be made of our trustee Neil Smith, that most accomplished historian, who has been researching our records for more than a decade. As a long-standing member of the Club, Neil more than anyone else has provided the greatest contribution to this volume.

We also owe a special debt of gratitude to Bernard Share for his professional involvement. Bernard has been a close friend for more than thirty years, and from the moment I put the proposition to him over lunch in the Club early last year I knew that we were on a winner.

Later, as the contributions began to drift in, I was struck by a notable common denominator — *The Members' Table*. I suppose that somewhere in the back of our minds we all realise that a very considerable amount of highly intellectual activity revolves around that Hub of the Hierarchy which at times can also produce such a delightful mixture of Humbug and Hilarity. But it wasn't until I started reading the various articles that I realised the full implications of that nerve centre situated in the left hand corner of the dining room.

One of the permanent patrons of that particular quarter tells us he 'often wished that he could record the coverage at the Members' Table'. He also mentions 'current affairs and historical events featuring regularly' and that 'a fly on the wall on some of these occasions would have been very privileged indeed.'

In a very humorous Rugger article we are told that on a Monday at lunchtime the Club Table is 'The place to be after any special sporting event – The British Open, Wimbledon, The Horse Show . . . Rugby International Weekends'. Another piece of contemporary coverage tells us about our share of club funny men and club bores and about one of the favourite table pastimes of selecting a Representative Cricket XI at many of 'these interesting after dinner sessions'.

In addition to the production of this Club History, it is worth recording a few of our special sesquicentennial activities for posterity. At the time of writing we have already held four exceptionally well supported functions. We celebrated Our Day at the Races in great style when sponsoring an £8,000 Hurdle at Punchestown. This was a most memorable occasion with well over three hundred members and friends sitting down to a Private Marquee Luncheon on Thursday 26th April, the final day of the National Hunt Festival Meeting.

Our Night at the Opera followed on Wednesday 2nd May when we arranged a block booking of the Dress Circle at the Gaiety Theatre for 142 supporters of 'Madame Butterfly' followed by a full house for supper in the Club.

Highlighting our summer schedule was the Sesquicentennial Luncheon on Monday 9th July. As Guest of Honour we had our own most distinguished member Dr. Patrick J. Hillery, President of Ireland, who was joined by two recent but very welcome additions to our ranks – the American and Canadian Ambassadors. This occasion marked the official re-opening of our Reading Room which was completely refurbished thanks to the benevolence of Tony O'Reilly and John Meagher.

Friday, 14th September, saw us travelling to the National Concert Hall for the Martinu Centenary and, once again, we rounded off the evening with another very enjoyable supper in the Club. All being well, it is intended that *Whigs on the Green* will be launched at our formal Sesquicentennial Dinner on 2nd November. This will be followed by our Gala Ball – a very unique occasion in the Club with Dancing in the Dining Room and table seating in the Reading Room, Drawing Room and Card Room throughout the evening. Finally we return to the Gaiety Theatre on Wednesday 5th December where the D.G.O.S. will entertain us with their presentation of 'Tosca'.

A selection of three sesquicentennial wines was specially bottled in France to celebrate this very special year and our Fontmure 1985, St Estèphe 1986 and St Véran 1988 are being very well received in their distinctive 'Stephen's Green Club' livery.

Everything connected with our Sesquicentennial and with the lead up to it has involved a great deal of effort from a great many people. Those of you who put pen to parchment in order to make this history possible are all essential ingredients in the Celebratory Cake but there were others who helped with the icing. I know very well that one of our renowned Club wags has cleverly suggested that we should 'avoid mentioning names as far as possible, for to include is to exclude,' and so I must ask those of you who have given me so much assistance, co-operation and – most of all – encouragement over the past few years to permit me to live dangerously for one solitary paragraph in which I feel bound to record my very special gratitude to a small representative handful from our entire membership.

Our current chairman, the genial Brian Price, has always been particularly supportive while the House Committee under the leadership of David Callaghan have shouldered a tremendous amount of responsibility in our refurbishment campaign. The infrequently used title of 'Father of the House' would rest appropriately on the shoulders of my confessor and revered trustee Paddy Brennan and finally I would like to put it on record that no chairman of the Club could ask for a more dedicated Secretarial ally than that tireless trooper Desmond H. O'Neill.

Let's hope that between us all — members and friends alike — in this our wonderful Sesquicentennial Year, we may leave behind a few footprints of encouragement . . . footprints that perhaps, at some time in the future, a forlorn or shipwrecked member seeing may take heart again!

Sincerely,

Chairman,
Sesquicentennial Sub-Committee
18th September 1990

St Stephen's Green and Plot No 28
T. AUSTIN DUNPHY

T. Austin Dunphy

Members of the Stephen's Green Club are very fortunate to have, as their seat, one of the finest 18th century town houses in Ireland, containing many features which are of European importance. In addition, it is situated on the best side of the earliest and largest of the Dublin Squares looking south over a delightful and historic park. Members are fortunate too in that they still occupy the premises where their club was founded and where, this year, they celebrate 150 years of continuous occupation. During that long period the Club initiated many alterations to the original house, as well as carrying out major additions to it. In this history it would seem appropriate to include brief notes on the history of the Square from which the Club takes its name and the house which has been its home for so long.

A few years ago when it seemed possible that, for financial reasons, the Club might have to abandon its old premises and move to a modern building it was heartening to see how the membership, almost to a man, rejected any idea of moving and set about finding ways to overcome the problems and initiate a programme of refurbishment which is now well under way. This unhappy period has at least one good side to it; it showed beyond doubt the affection in which this old house is held by the present generation members.

When Dublin expanded beyond the confines of the cramped medieval city it spread eastward towards Trinity College and northwards towards Oxmantown Green, which became a fashionable suburb. The area now occupied by St. Stephen's Green was a swampy, marshy area, remote from the city, inhabited by thieves, highwaymen and other undesirables. Its main interest as far as the citizenry of Dublin was concerned was that it was on the route to the gibbet which stood near Baggotrath Castle, not far away to the east. Public hangings were relatively common in those days and, provided *the* spectator sport of the period. People trailed happily down what is present day Baggot

11

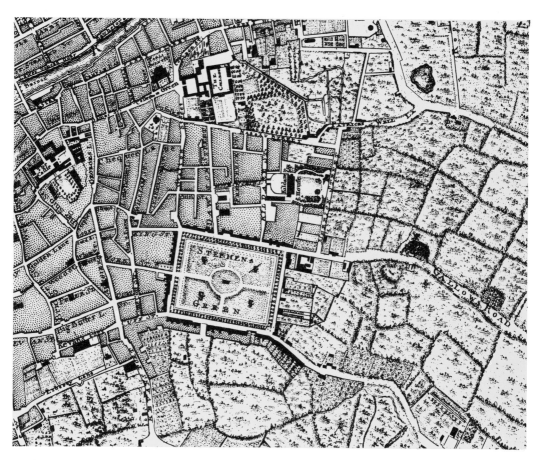

Roque's map of 1756
(National Trust Archive).

Street to witness the hanging of well-known criminals and it was generally regarded as a pleasant day out, much as their descendants trail down the same street today towards Lansdowne Road.

The 'Green' was first shown in undefined outline in Sir William Petty's *Down Survey* of Dublin and its environs of 1655. Towards the end of the century it was described as *Viridis Sancti Stephani* and was the property of the Dublin Corporation. It then consisted of some 60 acres which included the present St. Stephen's Green, together with the area of the sites of the later buildings which surrounded it. It remained, however, an unenclosed, marshy common. It was approached from the city by a lane joining the north-west corner (the present Grafton Street) and along the northside ran a road to Baggotrath Castle and the gibbet.

The Dublin Corporation had no money in 1663! *Plus ça change, plus c'est la même chose.* However, rather than putting an extra penny or so on the rates of their decayed and miserable city (as it then undoubtedly was) they hit upon the idea of developing their marshy, *Viridis Sancti Stephani* for building purposes. An assembly was held

12

that year which proposed that 'by reason of the late rebellion and long continued troubles of the Kingdom, the treasury of this city is clearly exhausted, and the yearly revenue thereof is reduced to little or nothing so that in all likelihood they will not be able to defray the public charge which must of necessity fall to them'. They further proposed that 'outskirts of St. Stephen's Green and other waste lands about the city, that now added nothing at all to pleasure or profit, may be set for 99 years, or to fee farm and a considerable rent secured'. Accordingly, in the following year, 1664, the Corporation marked out an area of about 27 acres to be preserved as an open space for the use of the citizens, and around it laid out about 30 acres for building, which was divided into strips or lots running back from the green with frontage to it of approximately 60 feet each.

The northside, which in fact extended beyond the present St. Stephen's Green, almost to the corner of Baggot Place, contained 33 lots; the southside contained 24 lots, on the east were 15 lots and on the west, 18; a total of 90 lots in all. The lots on each side were separately numbered in an anticlockwise direction so that, for instance, the Stephen's Green Club which is now no. 9 St. Stephen's Green was lot no. 28 on the northside; 86 St. Stephen's Green was lot no. 11 on the southside, and so on. For convenience we will use the modern numbering and where appropriate put the original plot number in brackets after it.

The plots were drawn by members of the Corporation and others and each allottee received a fee farm grant of his plot, and had to pay a small ground rent of one penny per sq.ft., for lots on the north, east, and west sides and one half-penny per sq.ft., for those on the south side; 'the fines for each lease to be applied to walling in and paving the Green for the ornament and pleasure of the City'. It was further laid down that each person who drew a lot should plant six sycamore trees near the wall to be erected around the Green, and that the houses which might be built on the lots were to be of brick, stone and timber, covered with tiles or slates and be at least two floors above the cellar. The Club occupies lot no. 28 on the north side and was originally allocated to Thomas Waterhouse, Alderman. There appears to have been some dealing in these allotments because, by 1729 the lease had been transferred to Joseph Leeson (father of the first Earl of Milltown, builder of Russborough, Co. Wicklow) who also held the lease of lot no. 27, and others as we shall see later. If my memory serves me correctly the Leeson family held this ground and indeed were ground landlords of the Club until well into this present century.

In 1666, one William Harvey was employed in 'ploughing up and levelling St. Stephen's Green' and in 1669 Edward Briscoe and Patrick Henderson were employed to build a four and a half foot high stone wall around the whole area. The following year trees were planted and pavements were laid. A ditch was dug to drain the still swampy land and between this ditch and the wall a 35 ft. wide lime tree-lined walk was laid out. Further hedge-lined walks occupied other parts of the Green. By 1671 the lane leading from Hoggen (College) Green, the present day Grafton Street, had become 'so foule and out of repair that persons cannot passe through the said Green for the benefit of the walks therein'. The Corporation immediately ordered its repair and improvement.

The ground rents of the lots around the Green were in 1670 passed to the Blue Coat School to pay for building maintenance and to provide an income for the School, but the interior of the Green remained the property of the City and was used for pasturage of the citizens' cattle and horses and, from very early times, as a place of assemblage for people on public occasions and for the muster and exercise of troops.

There are many accounts throughout the 18th century of celebrations held in the Green, one of the most elaborate the great Fireworks display of 1749 arranged to celebrate the general peace concluded at Aix-La-Chapelle. These fireworks were arranged under the direction of James Neville, the Surveyor General, and were on a most elaborate scale. The *Universal Magazine* for January 1749 describes the scene thus: 'In the centre was a 12-sided temple of peace, 64 ft. high and 32 ft. wide, illuminated from within, the sides adorned with statues. In the front of the 3 sides towards the west was Liberty, with Justice on the right and Fortitude on the left. In the Frieze over Liberty was a Medallion with Minerva sitting on a rock, holding a spear in her right hand, and in her left hand a mirror reflecting rays of light consuming instruments of war; and above this on the cornice a bust of King George II. On the north side was Science, with Liberty on the right and Prudence on the left; above, a medallion with the figure of Apollo pointing to the University of Dublin, and over this device a bust of the Prince of Wales. On the south the statues were Glory, Tranquillity, and Plenty. Over the figure of Glory a medallion with Hercules slaying Hydra, and, above, a bust of the Duke of Cumberland. On the east sides were Constancy, Concorde, and Clemency. Over the figure of Constancy was a medallion with a youth holding an open rose bud, the Rising Sun in the background; above this a bust of the Stadtholder of the United Provinces. Along the frieze were other emblems and on the cornice, 8 busts of eminent law givers and heroes. Over the temple, in which 1,100 yards of Persian silk was used, there was a gilt dome with a statue of Peace. The hall was enclosed in a space of 300 ft. square by a balustrade of large sockets interspersed with lighted obolisks and pillars, in magnificence and taste exceeding anything of the kind that has been exhibited in this kingdom'. Throughout the 18th century there were, however, military displays, concerts and, in 1763 the 'watchmen of the several parishes in the City, properly accoutered, in pursuance of the Chief Magistrate's order, marched to St. Stephen's Green and made a very formidable appearance'. In short, it became the focal point for mass entertainment in the City.

In 1752 the Corporation of Dublin decided to erect a statue of King George II, and tenders were invited from sculptors for the proposed work. Two designs were submitted by John Van Nost and one of these was accepted by the Council in July 1753. The statue was completed in 1756 at a cost of £1,000 exclusive of the pedestal, and was erected in the centre of the Green in 1758. The statue was erected on a large and most elaborate pedestal, twenty feet square, with a raised terrace all around it designed by an architect called Joseph Jarratt of whom we will hear more later. The well-known drawing by James Malton of 1797, a copy of which is in the Club, shows the statue standing in the centre of the Green on its elaborate base.

Unfortunately this statue, like that of King William III in College Green and later Lord Gough in the Phoenix Park by the Irish sculptor James Foley, was subjected to various attempted mutilations, and in the end all were destroyed by vandals of one type or another, leaving Dublin, which boasted three superb equestrian statues, with none.

The heyday of the Green as a fashionable promenading area coincided with the heyday of Dublin, that is, from the middle to the end of the 18th century. The walk along the northside known as Beaux' Walk was 'finer gravelled than the Mall' according to Swift. In 1771 it was described as 'a place of public resort especially on Sundays when the nobility and gentry take the air and parade in their carriages'. Lewis's *Dublin Guide* of 1787 records that 'in the walks may be seen, in fine weather, a great resort of company; the Beaux' Walk in particular being considered in the same light here as the Mall in St. James's Park, London – the scene of elegance and taste'.

In 1792 it was proposed to build a Mansion House for the Lord Mayor of Dublin in the centre of the Green which, reports a contemporary newspaper, 'would render our Lord Mayor's residence the most magnificent and striking of any magistral house in Europe'. However, the proposal was dropped following opposition from the citizens who were suspicious that such a move might deprive them of their beloved Green.

Malton's drawing of 1797 preserves the view of St. Stephen's Green at its most fashionable period. Alas, by 1814, a sad picture of decay is presented to us; 'the hedge was ragged and gapped, and the ditch covered in green duckweed, and here and there piles of soot and occasional dead cats and dogs; the double row of elm and lime trees, mostly gone'. The elegant promenade had given way to a scene of neglect and decay.

The principal entrance to the Green was originally on the west side opposite York Street, where stood a gateway of four piers of black stone, each surmounted by a granite ball. By 1818, this too was in a state of decay. However, in spite of this degradation, Beaux' Walk was 'still [in 1818] frequented in fine weather by the inhabitants of the "middle class" (sic) in the vicinity'. In Autumn and Winter it was used as a football ground for 'roughs and Liberty boys'.

Probably because St. Stephen's Green was unique among the 'Squares' of Dublin in being from the earliest times open to the citizens of Dublin, it has been held by them in great affection. It is therefore not surprising that there was much agitation and many abortive efforts to rescue it from its neglected state. At one time the Corporation who were, yet again, short of money, planned to develop part of the Green for further building; this plan was opposed and defeated by the inhabitants as they had already defeated the proposal to hand over the Square as a residence for the Lord Mayor. However, the government came to the rescue, and in 1814 an Act was put through parliament for the improvement of the Square. The preamble of this Act says 'whereas the Square called St. Stephen's Green in the City of Dublin, is become and must continue to be a very great public nuisance unless the present wet ditch, which encloses the interior of the said Square, be filled up and the said interior of the aforesaid Square be enclosed by a proper enclosure and otherwise improved'. Under this Act, Commissioners were appointed who obtained from the Corporation a fee farm grant of the Green at a rent of £300 p.a. They proceeded to level and drain the interior, form walks, plant trees and shrubs, remove such decayed and old trees as still survived, fill in the ditch, remove the wall which was built in 1669 and enclose the whole area in iron railings. At the same time the granite posts on the outside of the footpath, which still survive, but which originally had chains slung between them, were erected.

Although these improvements were welcome, they had very serious and important consequences. By enclosing the Green with iron railings and locked gates which could only be opened by householders paying a guinea a year for their keys, the Square became, in effect private property, shut off from the citizens of Dublin. Naturally this was very much resented and the citizens rightly objected at being deprived of their ancient rights to use the Green for their enjoyment, and many efforts were made to have the Green again open to the public. These efforts, however, were always opposed by the Commissioners and by the Dublin Corporation. However, in 1877 Sir Arthur E. Guinness, who was M.P. for the City, obtained an Act of Parliament under which the Green was again to be thrown open to the public and placed in the custody of the Board of Works, now the Office of Public Works, in whose care it still remains. Sir Arthur himself bore the cost of converting the marshy, flat, park into the beautiful garden we know today. His work in laying out the park was completed and the Green was formally restored to the people of Dublin in 1880. To commemorate the generosity of Sir Arthur Guinness (now raised to the peerage as Baron Ardilaun) the citizens of Dublin in 1892 erected a statue to him on the west side of the Green which still stands there today.

Let us now turn to the main object of this brief history – the home of the Stephen's Green Club, no. 9 St. Stephen's Green.

Members of the Club and others interested in the history of Dublin domestic architecture have long debated upon the origins of the present building: when was it erected, and how it developed into the building we know today.

In its original form it contained many unusual, even unique, features. For instance, it is entered from street level rather than by a large flight of steps leading to the entrance door as is the case in the other large houses on the north side of the Square. Even more unusual, the entrance was at the side of the house, approached through a porte cochère rather than on the street front. This writer is not aware of any other major Dublin house which had such feature. Why was this so?

This is a question which has never been fully addressed, so perhaps we could hazard a few guesses, based on a little detective work. Could it be so unusual because it is the oldest house on the Green, a lone survivor from the first, or early second generation of buildings?

Building work began on the plots allocated by the Dublin Corporation in 1664, almost immediately. Maurice Craig, in his classic book *Dublin 1660 to 1860* states that building was well advanced by 1685, especially on the north and west sides. Moll's Map of 1714 shows these sides completely built over but no building is shown on the east and south sides. However, notwithstanding this, we know that there were scattered buildings on the east side, at least. The Earl of Roscommon had his house here as early as 1686 and another large house, known as 'Spring Garden House' was there in 1711. Brooking's perspective view of 1728 shows three sides of the Green substantially built upon, but unfortunately this view is not orientated so we are not sure which side is which.

None of the early maps is sufficiently detailed to enable us to identify individual houses with any degree of confidence. We have to wait until 1756 when Rocque's Map was published to be able to recognise individual houses. Here No. 9 can be clearly seen, with its side entrance, its garden, and the slight setback behind No. 8, the present Hibernian United Services Club.

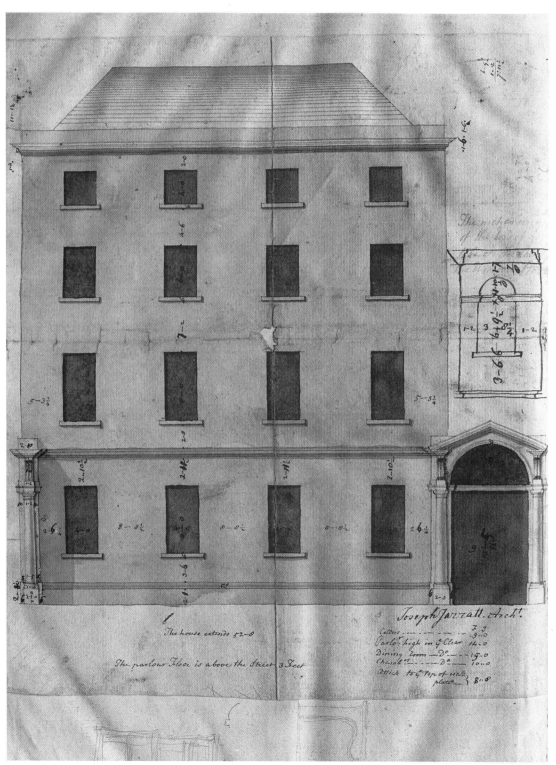

The Jarratt drawing, c1730. *(Irish Architectural Archive)*

Principally because of this map historians have tended to attribute a date of 1756 or a little earlier, to the building of No. 9 – a contributory factor possibly being that the Georgian Society Records of 1910 have been unable to trace any occupants of the house before 1757 when it was lived in by the Harman family.

The first house of importance on the north side, using the present numbering system, was on the site of No. 7 St. Stephen's Green, formerly 'Smiths of the Green, Wine Merchants and High Class Grocers'. In 1664 this site, plot No. 30, was leased by the Corporation to one Nathanial Foulks, a tailor, who transferred the lease to Abel Ram, of Ramsford, Co. Wexford who built a house on the site. In 1702 Ram leased this house to Edward, 4th Earl of Meath. It remained the town house of the Earls of Meath until they purchased their new house on the east side in 1775, but it continued to be occupied by the brother of the 8th Earl until 1794. It was pulled down by the Smiths to build their wine shop in 1830. The important point here is that a substantial house, suitable for the town house of a 4th Earl, was built before the end of the 17th century. The next house, No. 8, the present Hibernian United Services Club, occupies former plot No. 29 and was the site of a house known to have been built before 1685 when it was occupied by John Heath of Finglas, Co. Dublin. This house was described in 1751/1752 as 'a very convenient large house, with two coach houses, three large stables, other convenient out-offices, and a large garden; very fit for a nobleman or private gentleman'. This early house too was pulled down and the present one erected about 1770. On the east side of the Stephen's Green Clubhouse was another large house built on the site of present Nos. 10 and 11 St. Stephen's Green (former plot No. 27) and lived in by Brigadier Sir Thomas Prendergast, Baronet. He was killed in the battle of Malplaquet in 1709, so he probably resided there before the end of the 17th century. This house was demolished in the 19th century and replaced by two smaller houses, now Nos. 10 and 11.

We see therefore that substantial houses were erected on plots Nos. 27, 29 and 30, occupied today by Nos. 7, 8, 10 and 11 St. Stephen's Green, before 1700. It would seem very unlikely that plot No. 28, the St. Stephen's Green Club site, would have been vacant for almost 75 years while substantial mansions were erected on either side of it. We have noted above that this site was allocated in 1664 to Thomas Waterhouse who transferred his lease to Joseph Leeson in 1729, so that it was not a piece of derelict waste land. It must, therefore be assumed that a house was built on the site of No. 9 around 1685, or very shortly afterwards.

The question we must now address ourselves to, is whether the house built at the end of the 17th century is the present St. Stephen's

19

Statue of George II,
St. Stephen's Green

Green Clubhouse or does the Clubhouse incorporate any portion of the 17th century building.

We referred earlier to the architect, Joseph Jarratt, who designed the large and handsome pedestal for the Van Nost statue of George II which stood in the middle of St. Stephen's Green. Jarratt was first 'discovered' by Dr. Maurice Craig when researching his book *Dublin 1660 to 1860*, but little was known about him and he remained a shadowy figure on the fringes of the 18th century architectural world in Dublin. In the early 1980s an album of drawings and designs by Jarratt, together with plates from French and Italian books was discovered and acquired by the Irish Architectural Archive. In the Autumn 1984 edition of *The Irish Arts Review* an article appeared by the then Director of the Irish Architectural Archive, Nicholas Sheaff, entitled 'Jarratt and the Rococo', in which Sheaff suggests that Joseph Jarratt was a significant figure in 18th century Dublin architecture. Indeed, on the strength of Jarratt's signed drawings in the album he credits him with authorship of many important works formerly attributed to Sir Edward Lovett Pearce (1699 – 1733), the architect of the Old Parliament House, now the Bank of Ireland, and one of the greatest architects of the 18th century.

Among these buildings are the garden front of the State Apartments, Dublin Castle (1740); the 'Piano Nobile' also in the State Apartments, with its compartmented, toplit, corridor (1732); the La Touche Bank, Castle Street (1735 – 39); and some others. Although the only drawing in the album which has been actually dated is that of the pedestal for the George II statue in St. Stephen's Green (1756), the other buildings, especially those listed above can be dated fairly accurately and they all date from the late 1730s. He is also credited with the design of the Weaver's Hall which formerly stood in the Coombe, Dublin, which was built between 1745 and 1747.

It is clear then that Jarratt was working in one capacity or another from the early 1730s right on until he retired or died in 1774. The significance of Joseph Jarratt as far as our investigation is concerned is that among the contents of his album is an undated drawing of a large and grand house, which is undoubtedly an early design for No. 9 St. Stephen's Green. Although it differs in a number of important ways from the building actually erected it also has many similarities. The drawing is of a four bay, four storey over basement house, entered at street level through an arched and pedimented porte cochère on the east side. The original No. 9 St. Stephen's Green house was a five-bay, three-storey house, but the design of the porte cochère on the Jarratt drawing is almost identical with the porte cochère which existed in the Stephen's Green Clubhouse and which can be seen in the photograph of the Club taken in 1860. This porte cochère survived until the major refacing of the Club building and the addition of the mansard roof in the early part of this century. It would seem that the key to the dating of No. 9 St. Stephen's Green is to establish the period of Jarratt's active life.

Sir Edward Lovett Pearce, whose short life spanned the years from 1699 to 1733, died very unexpectedly while many of his projects were either building or on the drawing board. As Surveyor General for Ireland he, presumably, had a substantial architectural staff who would have continued his work after his death. He was succeeded as Surveyor General by Arthur Dobbs.[1] He was an administrator, not an architect, so there must have been some one architect who took charge of the actual architectural office and the building work on site. Could this person be Jarratt?

On the information available, there is no reason why he could not have been Pearce's assistant and near contemporary. This would account for the 'Pearcian' drawings in the album and the reason why many of

1. Arthur Dobbs, of Castle Dobbs, Carrickfergus, Co. Antrim; gentleman. Agriculturalist, astronomer, explorer. Founder member of the R.D.S. Governor of North Carolina. On his return to Ireland he greatly advanced the study of bees and their habits.

the buildings drawn by Jarratt were attributed to Pearce, i.e. because they were both working on these projects as principal and assistant.

Nicholas Sheaff, in his *Irish Arts Review* article, tends to move the dates of the buildings forward to suit the period when Jarratt was deputy Surveyor General, from 1753 to 1763. But this would be contrary to all evidence. For instance, Pool and Cash in their *Views of the most remarkable public buildings, monuments and other edifices in the city of Dublin* written about 1778, published in Dublin in 1780, describes the garden front of the State Apartments in Dublin Castle as 'modern' and ascribes a date of 1740 to it. If that building had dated from as recently as 1760s, surely these writers who were studying

Dublin buildings would have known about it and dated it accordingly?

This writer believes that Jarratt was active from at least 1730 until his retirement or death in 1774.

How does this affect our investigation of the date of the building of the Stephen's Green Club? The drawing of what we believe to be the original St. Stephen's Green Club is a simple, unsophisticated drawing and could have been the work of a young architect: it is suggested here that it dates from about 1730. It is the writer's suggestion that it was designed by Jarratt, probably for Joseph Leeson who took over the lease of the site, or the house, which stood on the site of the present Stephen's Green Club in 1729. When we come to describe the building in detail, mention will be made of a few points which will tend to support this view.

Joseph Leeson, described as 'an eminent brewer', was also a large property owner. As well as owning the building or site of No. 9 St. Stephen's Green, he also owned the site of the present Nos. 10 and 11 on the northside of the Green and a large block of property on the southside, at present occupied by the former Methodist Church and Nos. 92 to 98 inclusive. This block contained Leeson's dwelling house and his garden and a huge brewery at the rear. On his death in 1741 he left an estate of some £6,000 per annum and '£50,000 in money'. The 'eminent brewer's son', also Joseph, was MP for Rathcormack from 1742 to 1756 when he was raised to the peerage as Baron Russborough of Russelstown, Co. Wicklow. He became Earl of Milltown in 1763. The Earls of Milltown continued as landlords of the premises until well into this century.

Joseph Leeson never appears to have occupied No. 9 and it is not known for certain who resided in the house between 1730 and 1757, unless it was Wentworth Harman II who died in 1758 when his brother, the Rev. Cutts Harman was first registered as occupant. He resided there until he died in 1784 when his nephew and heir, Lawrence Parsons (created Baron Oxmantown in 1792 and Earl of Rosse in 1806) became occupant. The 2nd Earl of Rosse owned the house until 1812 when Peter La Touche (of the banking family) took over. In subsequent years it went through a rather rough period and seems to have been, for a short time at least, a boarding house. Sir Walter Scott's son was living there when his regiment was quartered in Dublin at the time of his father's visit in 1825. Lockhart's *Life of Scott* records: 'We reached Dublin in time for dinner, and found young Walter and his bride established in one of those large noble houses in St. Stephen's Green (the most extensive in Europe), the founders of which little dreamt that they should ever be let at an easy rent as garrison lodgings'.

In 1837, the house was taken over by the Union Club which, in the following year, was dissolved and later reconstituted as 'The Stephen's Green Club' who have remained there ever since.

The house shown on Jarratt's drawing does not seem to have been built, instead a five bay (i.e. five windows across the facade) three storey over basement house was erected, but Jarratt's unique feature of the side entrance via a porte cochère was retained. Also retained was the simple elevational treatment of the facade shown on Jarratt's drawing.

It is not very clear how the plan of the house worked in detail. There were undoubtedly two rooms along the front facade on both the ground and first floors. The second floor would have been very much as it is today, except for the projection at the rear of the building (the second floor bathroom and wc and the Ladies' Powder Room below it). The staircase may have finished on the second floor although there could have been an attic storey lighted by dormers prior to adding the mansard roof in 1901/2.

The rear portion of the ground and first floors present somewhat of a puzzle. Most large houses of the period had a principal staircase leading up to the first floor at least, and frequently to the second. They also had a secondary staircase, usually narrow and built of stone

One of the covered-up windows behind the staircase, designed c1730

elsewhere in the house. The present secondary staircase of the Club is far too large and prominent to fit into this subsidiary category. The present main staircase is one of the finest in Dublin, but it is probable that it was a later insertion. There are a number of reasons for suspecting this: (a) there are two covered-up windows behind the staircase which can still be seen from the outside of the building. They are both directly under the existing high, round-headed windows of the staircase, one under the first landing and partially concealed by the dado of the staircase, and the second over the entrance to the ground floor cloakroom, the upper part of this also concealed by the dado; (b) the arches over the existing windows of the stairhall, when viewed from the outside, are obviously of later constructions than the surrounding brickwork of the wall; (c) grand staircases rising directly from the entrance hall is a feature more common in large houses built in the later 18th century, although there are many exceptions to this general rule. Earlier houses had their staircases in separate compartments, examples being Clanwilliam House, St. Stephen's Green; Tyrone House, Marlborough Street; the Provost's House, Trinity College and Leinster House.

If this theory is correct, how was the house planned on the ground and first floors? On the ground floor there was probably a large single storey Entrance Hall entered from the porte cochère and leading on to the main staircase of the house which is now the secondary staircase. The upper part of the Stairhall would have been a reception room, matching the present Drawing Room and forming a suite of interconnecting rooms with the present Reading Room. It is interesting to note that there is a door, blocked up on the Reading Room side, but still visible at the top of the secondary staircase which would have led into the larger of the two rooms which at present make up the Reading Room. This would have been the principal entrance to the suite of reception rooms.

These alterations were probably carried out about 1756 to 1757 at the time when the Rev. Cutts Harman took up residence. He transformed the house from a large, but simple town house to a very grand mansion. He inserted the noble staircase and employed the Lafranchini brothers to create the superb rococo interiors we see today, interiors which are among the finest of their type in Europe.

Who were these superb artists who brought the rococo style of stucco work to Ireland, a style for which Dublin was to become famous? Up to recently we knew them as 'the Franchini Brothers', Paul and Philip: Italians who were brought to Ireland by the 19th Earl of Kildare in 1739 and who executed for him the famous ceiling in the Saloon (formerly the Dining Room) at Carton, Co. Kildare. In the last few years a considerable amount of research has been carried out into these stuccoists by Carlo Palumbo-Fossati, using archival documents from Ireland, England and Switzerland, which may be of interest.

The first point of note discovered was that their surname was not Franchini or Frankiney, as Lady Louisa Conolly of Castletown called them but Lafranchini, and, although they spoke Italian, they were not Italians but Swiss! They were among the 15 children of Carlo Lafranchini and Isabella Albutio from the small town of Bironico, ten kilometres north of Lugano, in the Italian-speaking part of Switzerland known then, as now, as 'Svizzera Italiana'. They were a prosperous, armigerous family whose coat of arms may still be seen in the parish church of Bironico. Although the family were sufficiently well-off, some of the sons had to find work outside the village and three brothers, Paul (Paola), Philip (Filippo) and Peter Noel (Pietro-Natale) became stuccoists. They were born in 1695, 1702 and 1705 respectively. All three went to England where they joined many other foreign artists working there and where they carried out a considerable amount of work. The two elder brothers, Paul and Philip, came to Ireland in 1739 on the invitation of the Earl of Kildare to work on Carton. Thereafter they carried out an enormous amount of wonderful work, notably Riverstown House, Co. Cork (copies of this work at present adorn Aras an Uachtaráin and there is a copy of one of the Riverstown panels (depicting 'Grammer' c.1740) in the Drawing Room of the Stephen's Green Club); Clanwilliam House, St. Stephen's Green; Tyrone House, Marlborough Street; Russborough, Co. Wicklow; Curramore, Co. Waterford; Castletown, Co. Kildare and many, many town houses. It is not known for certain whether both brothers worked on the Stephen's Green Club but certainly Philip did and it is more than likely that he was joined as usual by his brother, Paul.

Paul and his younger brother, Peter Noel, who had been working in England for most of his life, returned to Switzerland about 1770, Paul dying there in 1776 and Peter Noel in 1788. Philip remained in Ireland where he died in June of 1779.

The Lafranchini brothers ushered in the great period of rococo plasterwork in Ireland and it was not long before Irish craftsmen learned the technique of modelling figures, trophies, fruit and flowers. The use of moulds was limited and most of the modelling had to be done by hand *in-situ*. The angle of a bird's neck, the choice of flowers in reed or garland, a cloak blowing in the wind, are personal touches which helped to imprint the style of the artist on his work. There is, as Desmond Guinness points out in his *Irish Rococo Plasterwork* a somewhat static quality in Lafranchini's heavily stylised figures enclosed in their bolection frames which makes them easily recognisable.

Many people have commented on the striking similarity between the plasterwork in the Stephen's Green Club and that in Castletown House, particularly the staircases, which are almost identical in detail, although in the case of Castletown, on somewhat larger scale. There are other similarities also with Castletown House in that in Castletown, although the house was completed substantially by 1722, the staircase was not put in until 1759/60: in other words in both cases the grand staircases were inserted after the houses were substantially completed.

Armed Minerva with attributes. Detail from ceiling in large drawing-room. *(Irish Architectural Archive)*

The rococo work in Stephen's Green Club is generally regarded as among the finest in Dublin and is of European importance. Here again, the question of dating crops up. C. P. Curran, in his splendid book *Dublin Decorative Plasterwork of the 17th & 18th Centuries* (London 1967) records that there was some doubt among architectural historians that the Lafranchini were responsible for the work because it was believed that they had returned to 'Italy' by the mid-1750s, i.e. after the date given in the Georgian Society Records, for the building of No. 9 St. Stephen's Green. However, this was put right by the discovery of a letter dated May 1759 written by Lady Louisa Conolly of Castletown to her sister, the Countess of Kildare, in which she says 'Mr. Conolly and I are excessively diverted at Franchini's (sic) impertinence, and if he charges anything of that sort to Mr. Conolly, there is a fine scold in store for *his* Honour'. This shows that the Lafranchini, or one of them, was working in Castletown in mid-1759. We now know that one of the brothers remained permanently in Ireland while the other remained here until about 1770. Because of the great similarity between the stucco work in the two buildings, it is clear that they were both executed about the same time, the Stephen's Green Club work being about three years or so earlier.

How is one to describe the Lafranchini stucco work in the Stephen's Green Club? It is to be seen in three parts of the house; the staircase; the Dining Room, originally two separate rooms – a large and a small room; and the Reading Room, also originally two separate rooms – large and small.

To quote C. P. Curran: 'The staircase hall carries the early type of shell and swag decoration with masks and medallion busts, and there are three classical subjects on wall panels in Louis XIV frames, including (on the south wall) the metamorphosis by Juno (shown complete with her peacock) of Antigone, the sister of Priam, into a stork'. This panel was no doubt included to warn wayward husbands. The legend has it that Juno's husband, Jupiter, was paying more attention than was 'proper' to Antigone who did not exactly reject his advances. Juno sorted the problem out by turning the unfortunate Antigone into a stork! Why a stork? Fortunately few members' wives possess Juno's powers: still, one can never be too careful!

On the west wall is a panel depicting the goddess Minerva, complete with shield, spear and helmet, lying on the clouds reaching out to an armed warrior.

The third panel, on the east wall, shows Mercury, the messenger of the gods, complete with winged helmet and caduceus, conveying a love message (see winged Cupid with an arrow at the bottom of the panel) to a beautiful draped girl with flowing veil in her hair. This could be a companion piece to the first panel, and the beautiful girl Antigone receiving a love message via Mercury from Jupiter? It is sad to think that she will end up as a stork in the not too distant future.

All of the wall panels are enlivened by a landscaped background which adds great interest to the subjects, but they lack the movement and variety of the ceilings in the main rooms which we will now now discuss.

Curran describes the ceilings in the Dining Room thus; 'In the large Dining Room (i.e. the larger portion of the present Dining Room) is a jolly Triumph of Bacchus (the god of Wine) involving ten putti. The Infant Bacchus armed with his thyrsus and leaning on a little barrel is pushed and drawn along in his triumphal rams-headed cart among the putti, drunk and hilarious, riot with trumpet and wine cups in the clouds'. Surrounding the centre-piece is a wonderful display of intertwined foliage, beautifully modelled with graceful and flowing lines. The smaller portion of the Dining Room, originally probably a Morning Room, has another centre-piece of putti in the clouds, this time holding garlands of roses and again surrounded by graceful swags, beautifully worked and intertwined. The garland of roses probably reflects the use of the room as a Morning Room, i.e. fresh and bright.

The cornices and outer surrounds to both of these areas, together with the beam supported by eagles or dragons which replaced the wall dividing the two original rooms date from 1841 when the two rooms were thrown into one.

The Reading Room is again an amalgamation of two separate rooms, corresponding to the rooms on the ground floor. The smaller portion has a superb ceiling showing a winged, reclining figure of Fame, with her trumpet, oak leaves and with her attendant putti on the clouds. Arranged round her are four episodes represented by putti, in one a child King, complete with crown entertains a petition; in the second, an infant Mercury with attendant Putti, bearing his caduceus, pours coins and fruit upon the earth. In another, Wisdom appears with mirror and serpent, and lastly, a personification of Liberty, his cap being placed on his head, enfranchising a slave. The whole beautifully worked in high relief.

The larger portion of the Reading Room has as its centre-piece another reclining figure, this time Fortitude with flowing drapes and cascading hair, armed with helmet, shield and uplifted sword (note how the sword is modelled separately, standing proud of the ceiling), attended by Putti, one pushing her cloud along, one about to shoot a threatening lion with an arrow from his bow and one straddling a tower emerging from the clouds. The centre group is surrounded by more garlands of flowers and leaves, cornucopiae of fruit, rocaille, stylised monsters and birds, connecting up eight groups representing the seasons and the elements, again in the form of putti. The seasons occupy the main axis of the ceiling with a charming Winter showing a putto wrapped around with drapes and a hood, warming himself over a fire. Spring is represented by a putto, holding garlands and flowers, Summer a putto with bunches of grapes and Autumn, by a putto with a sickle and a wreath on his head, representing the harvest.

Ceiling of smaller drawing room. *(Irish Architectural Archive)*

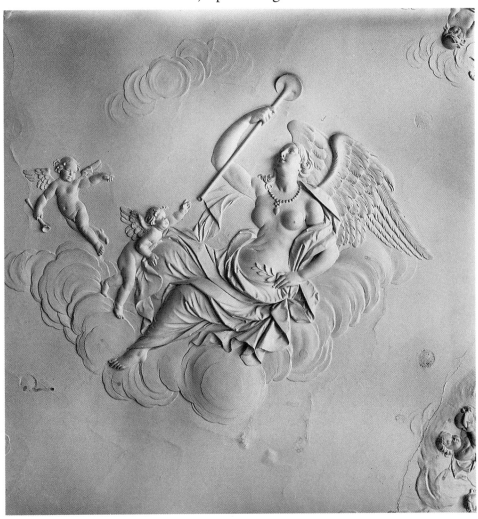

29

Summer a putto with bunches of grapes and Autumn, by a putto with a sickle and a wreath on his head, representing the harvest.

In the four corners the elements earth, water, air and lightning are represented by putti in different forms – for instance, air is represented by a putto mounted on an eagle, earth by a putto with a tower in its right hand and a key in its left, and so on.

All of us have dined and read under these beautiful works of art for years; we have passed them as we climb and descend the staircase, but how many of us have really looked at them and studied them as we would if they were paintings. Yet, this is an art of the highest quality, almost entirely modelled *in-situ* from wet plaster upside down on the ceiling. Few moulds were used in the early rococo plasterwork unlike the later Adam style of decoration which is largely pre-moulded. The subjects used are drawn from classical legends and sources such as Cesare Ripa's *Iconologia* published in Rome in 1593 and the great field of Italian and French art of the Renaissance. We are custodians of works of art equal in their way to any in the world. It is our responsibility to protect this and to hand it on to future generations. One thing is certain, the world is never again likely to see stucco work of this quality.

Part of larger dining room ceiling. *(Irish Architectural Archive)*

Although undoubtedly the Club's greatest treasure is its rococo stucco work, it can boast some other fine objects. The most obvious is the great staircase, dating from about 1756, one of the most beautiful timber staircases in Ireland. Many will have noticed the beautiful ram's horn scroll of the handrail at the bottom of the staircase, almost entirely carved from one piece of timber. Nowadays we could not even get the timber to make it, let alone the craftsmen to set it out and carve it. In 1983 this staircase, which was by then almost 230 years old, began to show signs of weariness. The Club initiated major repairs and large sections of the staircase were dismembered and the weaker parts strengthened and rebuilt. While this work was being carried out the opportunity was taken to remove layers of paint from the balusters and treads and from the finely carved spandrels and the frieze under the landing. The stairs now is fit for another 200 years, given reasonable attention. How many and varied the feet that have trod these steps over the past 234 years!

The Club also possesses some very distinguished chimneypieces, in particular the chimneypiece on the west wall of the Dining Room in grained off-white marble which could be from the original 'Jarrett House'. At the other end of the Dining Room is a smaller chimneypiece which again, could have come from the original house, but when the two rooms were thrown into one, this chimneypiece was increased in size by the addition of a carved timber piece set around it to bring it up to the scale of the now fairly large room. Both of these chimneypieces were disfigured, presumably in the early part of this century, when cast iron grates were installed but, during the 1982 re-decoration of the Dining Room, these were removed and more suitable grates substituted.

There is also a very beautiful Chinese Chippendale carved timber chimneypiece, dating from around 1760. This is at present in the Card Room but it is much earlier in date than the room so that it must have been moved there from somewhere else. Could it have been removed from the present kitchen/servery which, in the original house would have been an important room? This carved chimneypiece is shown in the Georgian Society Records with its original late 18th century grate, which has, alas, now disappeared. When funds become available it will be well worthwhile removing the layers of paint which are at present clogging up the fine detail of the carving and putting back a grate of the correct date. There is another good chimneypiece in the Entrance Hall which again could have survived from the 'Jarrett House' and a late 18th century Siena marble chimneypiece in the Drawing Room. The latter was cleaned and restored in 1988.

As mentioned earlier, the Stephen's Green Club was founded and took up occupancy at no. 9 in 1840. Almost immediately the Club

Part of smaller dining room ceiling

began adapting the house to render it suitable for its new purpose. The architect chosen to supervise the work was Michael Bernard Mullins, J.P. C.E. He was the son of Henry Mullins who appears to have practised as an architect under the title of Henry Mullins and McMahon, 1 Fitzwilliam Street, Dublin. Michael B. Mullins was originally apprentice to an eminent English surgeon but later switched to engineering, eventually becoming President of the Institution of Civil Engineers of Ireland in the period 1858 to 1861. He died at his house, 18 Fitzwilliam Square in July 1871.

The first work undertaken by Mullins in 1841 was to remove the wall dividing the two main front rooms on the ground floor. In doing so, he had to form a beam, spanning across the room from wall to wall, without pilasters. The ends of the beam are carried on a pair of eagles or dragons, one on either side of the room. Whether these have any structural significance or are purely decorative, is not clear. The original cornice and frieze in the two rooms were, for some reason, removed and early Victorian ones substituted in their place. The underside of the new beam was similarly decorated in early Victorian plasterwork. The room thus formed was described as 'the Coffee Room', a term still used in many London clubs to describe the 'Dining Room'. At this time too, presumably, the alterations referred to earlier to the chimneypiece on the east wall would have been carried out.

By 1844 the Club had obviously prospered because a large extension of nine additional rooms, including two billiard rooms, a large room referred to as the 'Smoke Room' (presumably a smoking room, but now the present Card Room) and four bedrooms were added. This extension, larger on plan than the original house, was connected to it by a short corridor. Bernard Mullins was again the architect.

In 1845, Mullins arranged for the two first floor rooms to be thrown into one to form the present Reading Room. It was he who was probably responsible for installing the two matching chimneypieces in the Reading Room and also for blocking up (on the room side) the original entrance door to the larger of the two first floor drawing rooms. This appears to have been the last work undertaken by Mullins for the Club.

Very little seems to have happened during the remainder of the 19th century as far as the building was concerned, any work which was carried out merely involved changing the use of various rooms. For instance, one of the billiard rooms, that to the east of the building, was converted into what was called the Strangers' Room, presumably the Guest Room, and the two windows in the east wall were formed. This room eventually became the Card Room and in 1928 adopted its present use as a bar. The large room referred to on the drawings as the 'Smoke Room' was used as a smoking room which accounts for the high ceiling with the ventilated roof light. The Victorians were just as conscious as we are today of the unpleasant aspects of smoking and it was permitted in the 'Smoke Room' and in the 'Coffee Room' at certain times only. In 1893 the Entrance door to this room was changed from the centre of the east wall to its present position and I would imagine, at the same time, the decorative plaster wall panelling was put in place. It remained as a smoking room until it was changed to the Card Room in 1928, when the present Members' Bar was formed from the then Card Room. There was a large staircase where the present Guest Bar and adjoining corridor now is, which was removed in 1913 and replaced by a room called 'The Lounge' which occupied the space of the present Guest Bar and the corridor outside it. It assumed its present form about 1950.

The next major project undertaken by the Club, the building of the third floor with its mansard roof and dormers, and the complete refacing of Jarratt's house to give the Club its present appearance, was carried out about the turn of the century. Unfortunately no record survives giving the exact date of this work, or of the architect who designed it. Drawings prepared by Mr. William H. Byrne, Architect, dated May/June 1902 (kindly lent to me by Mr. Byrne's great-great-nephew and Club member, Mark Leonard) make no mention of the refacing of the facade, although they do show a third floor plan with the front wall (where the mansard roof should be) erased, as though they were not quite sure what to draw. This poses somewhat of a problem. Was the refacing already done, or yet to be done? Was the mansard roof on, or not? If it was on, why was it not shown on the 1901/1902 drawings and if it was not, how could there have been a third floor? Unless new evidence comes to light, we have no definite

No. 9 St. Stephen's Green, photograph by William Garner. *(Irish Architectural Archive)*

answer to these questions. What is certain however, is that the building achieved its present appearance before 1905, and it is probable that the work was carried out by William H. Byrne & Sons, Architects.

The minutes of the late 19th and early 20th century record improvements in the staff accommodation, the installation of indoor plumbing and sanitary facilities, the installation of electric light, telephone, etc., but nothing of any architectural significance. There is a rather amusing drawing, prepared by W.H. Byrne & Sons and dated June 1940, showing details of how the basement was to be strengthened for use as an air-raid shelter. All the basement windows were protected with sandbags and the basement floor had an anti-shrapnel lobby, formed of sandbags. It illustrates, rather touchingly, another potential crisis in the life of this old building.

Virtually nothing was done to the fabric of the building over the last 50 or 60 years. Even routine maintenance was neglected. It was recently discovered that the last time the dormer windows on the top floor facing St. Stephen's Green, were painted was in 1948 – forty two years ago! By the late 1970s and into the early '80s the Club was in a most shabby and decrepit condition, but what was not appreciated by the majority of members was that the structure of the building had deteriorated to an almost dangerous state. One had the impression that the membership had almost despaired of ever being able to push back the tide of decay. However, in 1982, the Dining Room was redecorated and refurnished, and this seemed to put heart into some members, and looking back over those years, one could place this as the beginning of the renaissance in the fortunes of the building. In 1983 the staircase was repaired, in 1988 the Drawing Room was redecorated and refurnished, and shortly afterwards two bedrooms were refurbished, redecorated and refurnished. Restoration really got under way however, at the end of 1989, when major repairs to two sections of the roof of the building was put in hands, just in time, as it turned out, to stop a major dry rot outbreak from attacking the ceilings of the Reading Room. Hopefully, next year the Club will be able to complete the last section of the roof, which will ensure that this essential part of any building would be safe and secure for 100 years more.This year, our sesquicentennial year, our most beautiful room, the Reading Room was redecorated and is now more attractive than it has been at any time since the Rev. Cutts Harman transformed the house in 1757. In addition three further bedrooms on the second floor are being restored. And this impetus will ensure that the restoration of the building as a whole should be completed within the next few years.

This is a happy note on which to end this brief history of no. 9 St. Stephen's Green.

In the Beginning: 1837-1875

CORNELIUS F. SMITH

Cornelius F. Smith

A child described lace as 'gaps tied together with thread'. The many gaps in this historical essay have been connected, as best I can, by threads of fact and conjecture. Let us suppose that some leisured Club member stood gazing out through a window of the beautiful library of 'Number 9', and let his stream of consciousness flow idly over the scene and through the books around him. There would result an eclectic history of the Club as reflected in literature concerning Irish society and the clubs for its gentlefolk. Some of the topics which might well flow through our Clubman's mind would probably include:

some pictures of the Green and its denizens;

a swathe of history from the eighteenth century onwards;

the Club's formation and men who influenced it;

the Letters Patent of 1840; what did that signify?

How did other such clubs fare?

Surely it is good for us all – members and 'strangers' alike – to be familiar with the richness of the Club's heritage. It is a significant microcosm of the development of Irish society. The Chronological Table is intended to provide a view of history as seen through a squint-hole of the Club (See p. 190).

There has always been a special relationship between the Stephen's Green Club and its clubhouse. It is rather like having an extravagant mistress – who delights us with her whims but may bankrupt us in the end. She is part of our lifestyle in a very personal way. All our yesterdays gather around us here in this romantic old clubhouse.

Malton's beautiful print of the scene across the Beaux' Walk is a fine bench-mark for a survey of the area.

The view from the Club now shows two historic structures on the Green Parkscape: the memorial arch to the men of the Royal Dublin Fusiliers who died in the Boer War. Built in 1907, derisively nick-named 'The Traitors' Arch'; the fountain, with two horse troughs, presented by Lady Laura Grattan in 1880. Most of the numerous such conveniences erected by The London Metropolitan Drinking Trough Association have disappeared. It is mentioned by Samuel Beckett in *The End*. His father, William, was a member of the Club.

THE FORMATION
The first Committee of the Union Club (February 1837) included some 'volunteers' from the Viceroy's entourage:

Barron, Capt. John	A.D.C. – Gentleman at large
Bernal, Capt. Ralph	A.D.C.
Burke, Capt. Thomas J.	A.D.C.
Connellan, Cory	Gentleman at large
Fitzroy, Henry Esq.	Gentleman at large
Henkey, Major	8th Hussars
Higgins, Captain	HUSC Committee also
Quill, Lt. Colonel	HUSC Committee also
Sheridan, Francis Esq.	Gentleman of the Bed Chamber
Synge, Colonel	See Biographies 1.
Vaughan, Hon. Capt. George	Master of the Horse

Ulster King of Arms (Sir William Beham) regulated the fantastic ceremonial events at the Viceregal Court:

Full dress, for Drawing Rooms and State Balls;

Levée dress, for Dinners;

Undress, at Chapel Royal;

Blue Evening Dress and Cocked hat, A.D.C. not in waiting at Balls and Dinners.

These were honorific appointments without remuneration or power but did serve to groom a rising officer for future postings in the Empire: a retinue of chamberlains, comptrollers, secretaries and pages etc. also served to stand and wait. These Aides-de-Camp etc. were members of the Court of the Viceroys of Ireland. Daniel O'Connell admired 'Ireland's scrap of royalty' because it was a symptom of Ireland's independent existence as a Kingdom. Frequently Viceroys such as Mulgrave and Ebrington were liberal reformers to the discomfiture of the Kildare Street and Sackville Street Club members.

O'Connell and three of his four sons joined the Union Club in 1837. It was the golden age of reform in Ireland. The Union Club which originally met at Cumberland House on Pall Mall was extremely fashionable when founded in 1800. It continued, more soberly, at Trafalgar Square. Was there an association with the Dublin 'Union Club' 1837–9 which was the precursor of The Stephen's Green Club?

The name 'Union Club' may have been partly influenced by the long-established non-political Union Club in London rather than by a specific objective of perpetuating the Act of Union. However, in 1824

The Lady Laura Grattan fountain, St. Stephen's Green, 1880.
(Drawing: Pat Liddy)

it was the hard-line Sir 'Orange' Peel who opened their new club-house on Trafalgar Square. This hardly suggested any political tolerance of Reform, much less of Repeal.

The Master of the Horse was responsible for the proper care of his Excellency's horses, carriages and stables. When called upon, the Commissioners of Public Works (1831) were ever ready to maintain the Viceregal Lodge, the Castle and the Courts. The Aides-de-Camp were responsible for communication with the R.I.C., Army, Navy, the Transport authorities as well as with the Press. The arranging of the 'snob order' at dinners etc. was important in a court full of jobbery, place hunters, office seekers, briefless Barristers and younger sons without talent.

George Moore's sharply observed novel *Drama in Muslin* depicts the viceregal 'Drawing Room' in its decadence, where these potential husband/fortune hunters and place seekers vie in selfish ostentation. That world was crumbling before the rising tide of the Land War and Home Rule. Moore was not well loved by his class-conscious fellow members for his description of 'the pot-headed gigmen' of the Kildare Street Club.

Both the members of the Union Club and of its successor would have accepted the definition of a club as being 'a private house where gentlemen of like mind meet for relaxation and social intercourse'. However, 'like mind' would have involved a strong political bias. The Union members wanted the Act of Union to work fairly. The O'Connellites were far more radical reformers.

THE STEPHEN'S GREEN CLUB

In the absence of the Club's Minute Books, prior to 1875, we can only hazard a guess as to the scenes following the last General Meeting of the Viceroy's Union Club in February 1839. The first Stephen's Green Club General Meeting elected the new Committee in May 1840 to formalise the take over by the radical repealers led by Daniel O'Connell. No doubt there were 'whigs on the Green', but never a word to the newspapermen. However, the granting of H.M. Letters Patent (see Appendix II) signed in July 1840 does not indicate any Viceregal animosity to the new regime. No reference to the Club or the Letters Patent has been traced in the State Papers.

ORIGINAL MEMBERS

The lists of Committee members from 1837 onwards have survived (See p. 185). The names newly elected in 1840 tell the tale of a rising Irish middle class who sought independence or, at least, liberal reform. Study of these lists indicated that there was a considerable degree of identity between the membership of The Union Club and its successor The Stephen's Green Club.

Dr. Edward Hudson,
by W. Cuming
(National Gallery)

It is reasonable to suppose that Daniel O'Connell's 'Household Brigade' in the House of Commons would have used the Club circa 1840.

Sons	Maurice	1803–53
	Morgan	1804–55
	John	1810–58
	Dan (young)	1816–97 – not an M.P. until 1846

Sons in Law   Christopher Fitz-Simon who married Ellen
(also his brother Nicholas, M.P. "Fat Simon")
Charles O'Connell – married Kate

Brother in Law   William F. Finn

Cousins   Herbert Baldwin – first cousin
Domick Ronayne – distant cousin, close croney.

O'Connell's 'Tail' at the House of Commons included thirty-six pledged Repealers whose political interests would have drawn them to the liberal discussions in the reading room at the new club.

It is sometimes suggested that the Club was formed by gentlemen who had been blackballed by the Kildare Street Club. There is no documentary evidence of this story. Perhaps it is an echo of the rejection of the Right Hon. William Burton Conyngham and his friends by the jealous members of Daly's Club in 1781. However, it is circumstantially true that few of the original members 1837–40 would have escaped a blackball at the hands of the conservative/Unionist landowners at Kildare Street. There was no congenial room there for liberal Irishmen of Home Ruler outlook during the fierce political struggles which characterised the period between Catholic Emancipation and the Great Famine.

THE DUBLIN SCENE

The half century from the Act of Union until after the Famine was a drab period in Dublin. Life was unhealthy politically, economically and artistically. The landlords and parliamentarians had departed to London leaving behind the unfashionable and decaying post-Georgian city. The Industrial Revolution damaged Dublin's handcraft industries more than the potato blight did.

Club life was an antidote to boredom for H.M. Army and D.M.P. officers at the United Services or the dons and divines at the University Club. Increasingly the new upperclasses filled the vacuum. The local lawyers, doctors and merchants needed the new Stephen's Green Club

The Lord Lieutenant's reception and promenade, 7 June 1856 *(Illustrated London News)*

which was liberal-nationalist in politics and non-sectarian in religion.

An important function of the Club in the decades after 1837 would have been the provision of a newsroom with files of the London newspapers. Prior to the removal of stamp duty in 1855 and distribution by railways, most Dubliners would not have subscribed to newspapers, preferring to avail of 'newsrooms'. The circulation of the Dublin newspapers did not become influential until the second half of the last century.

More democratic municipal elections made Dublin's City Council a forum for increasingly Catholic and Nationalist ideas. The Liberals, supported by O'Connell, were in power during these formative years. It was Melbourne and Russell who appointed the well-meaning Lords Lieutenant Mulgrave and Ebrington.

The first decades of this liberal Club's existence saw that the wholly justified and necessary reforms in the administration of Ireland were doggedly resisted and delayed by Tory/Unionist politicians and the Established Churchmen. Catholic Emancipation, and the reforms of land tenure and of the electoral franchise, were withheld until they appeared to be forced out of Parliament only by threats of physical violence. The mythology of the Fenians and the I.R.A. is a living legacy of the British policy of 'too little and too late'. The Club stood for middle class liberalism and home rule by parliamentary procedures.

One can only surmise as to the extent to which Members understood the Irish language in pre-Famine times. Presumably some of the Club's servants were Irish speakers. However, the language was already in rapid decline even in the Wicklow Mountains. Daniel O'Connell spoke Irish but his influence was towards the unromantic, but pragmatic, concentration on English in the schools.

RELIGION IN CLUBLAND

Although the Club was founded a decade after Catholic Emancipation, religion was still a complex and burning issue in Dublin.

The Church of Ireland was still by law established, collecting its hated tithes and protecting its ascendancy power bases at the Bank of Ireland, Chamber of Commerce etc.

Evangelicals such as Archbishop William Magee encouraged "The New Reformation" of 1822–1860. Our ecumenical Edward Gustavus Hudson (q.v.) was exceptional.

Non-conformist churches were socially second rate although successful in business life.

The Catholics were thrusting upwards in the professions and trades. There were now 'jobs for the boys' under Daniel O'Connell and the Liberals. Many were educated by the Jesuits at Clongowes (1814) or in England.

41

The atheism professed by Wolfe Tone and some United Irishmen was no longer fashionable.

The omission of 'Saint' from The Club's name had little to do with ecumenicism. The Dublin street directories all were 'un-sainted' at that time.

The Stephen's Green Club was for Irish liberals of parliamentary reforming outlook. Hence – unlike the other clubs – the early committees show a reasonably balanced religious representation. The position of Jews in Dublin c. 1840 is referred to in the biographies of Rosenthal and Bernal.

Until after 1923 major business and financial institutions were controlled by the largely Church of Ireland/Unionist Ascendancy. However, this atmosphere would have been uncongenial, if not downright hostile, to the dissenting Protestant denominations who struggled to gain acceptance in the Dublin Chamber of Commerce.

No doubt this would have influenced a Presbyterian such as that great pioneer of professional accounting Sir Robert Gardner who joined the Club in 1887, his son John, and his partner George Hill Tullock. Judge James Owen Wylie (1885) was another example. The Society of Friends, known as 'Quakers', was well represented by important names such as Pim, Jonathan Hogg and Richard Grubb.

THE O'CONNELL CONNECTION

What can one usefully say about Daniel O'Connell (1775–1847) 'The Liberator' – the towering figure of European history whose bust graces our magnificent staircase? Not only was he an originating member of The Stephen's Green Club but also a club member at:

The Reform, on Pall Mall;
the Friendly Brothers
and the Freemasons.

O'Connell wrote to P.V. Fitzpatrick from the House of Commons on 20 November 1837: 'also pay at the Club in Stephen's Green the entrance and subscription of my sons and my own'. O'Connell and three of his four sons had joined the Union Club in 1837.

No doubt a take-over of the Union Club was part of O'Connell's unsuccessful Repeal Association which he launched in April 1840. By then the Whig/Liberal Government of Lord Melbourne (Prime Minister 1834–41) was nearing its end. The Irish Party had agreed to support it in exchange for Government appointments and reforms. Now was the time to organise political pressure from Ireland. His beloved wife Mary had died the previous year leaving him with few intimate friends.

Modern historians such as Kevin B. Nowlan, Oliver MacDonagh and Maurice O'Connell have reached the conclusion that O'Connell

The duel between Daniel O'Connell and D'Esterre, 1815 *(Irish Magazine)*

never regarded Repeal as practical politics in his own lifetime. 'Repeal' was just a loosely defined slogan which served as a continuous rallying-cry. It served as a stick to beat jobs and reforms out of the 'Orange Peel' Government from 1841 until the Great Famine of 1845. Unfortunately its increasingly clerical support did fuel real fears of 'Home Rule' in Ulster.

The Kerryman and the young Queen shared a surprisingly mutual admiration. This enraged *Punch* and the Irish Tory press.

It is interesting to observe here the tenacious life of O'Connell's pragmatic political credo. Yet elsewhere, his reputation has suffered at the hands of more romantic forms of Irishisms. I dare say that, by and large, most members of the Club today would still support his election manifesto:-

Government by a reformed democratic parliament with justice for Ireland. A Monarchy would not be incompatible with Home Rule for all Ireland.

There should be separation of Church and State.

Trade Unions were acceptable in principle – provided they were non-violent and did not act in restraint of free trade.

Opposition to:-
    Bloodshed (Civil War, duelling and faction fights)
    Gaelic culture (no practical use in modern world)
    Slavery
    Anti-semitism

Morgan O'Connell (1804–85) was elected to the Stephen's Green Club committee in May 1840, 1841 and 1842. The second son of the 'Liberator', he was born at 30 Merrion Square Dublin on 31 October 1804. He was educated at Clongowes Wood College 1815–1819. He enlisted in Irish South American Legion to aid Bolivia and then saw further military service in Austria. Returned to Ireland and became MP for Meath 1831–1840. Resigned in 1840 in disagreement with his father's Repeal policy and was appointed to Registry of Deeds at £1,200 a year, holding the post until 1868. Fought duel with Lord Alvanley on behalf of his father in 1835. Neither was hurt. In same year declined challenge from Disraeli. Died at 12 St. Stephen's Green Dublin, 20 January 1885. He was a man of modest ambitions and abilities.

THE CASTLE RULERS

The politically appointed officers of the British Government in Ireland at the time the Club was formed were:

Viceroy	–	Mulgrave (Phipps)	1835–39
Viceroy	–	Ebrington (Fortesque)	1839–41
Chief Secretary	–	Morpeth	1835–41
Under-Secretary	–	Drummond	1835–40
		MacDonald	1840–41

Thackeray forthrightly declared 'the old humbug of a Castle' to be 'the greatest sham of all the shams in Ireland'! However, many members of the Club were eager to receive viceregal invitations.

LONDON SETS THE PACE

The London clubs – and their imitations throughout the Empire – flourished during Victoria's reign:

Political Clubs	– Tory – Carlton +	Kildare Street
	– Liberal – Reform +	Union/Stephen's Green
	Brooks (1764)	Club – despite controversy, Daniel O'Connell and Tom Moore remained on as members.
Services	– East India	HUSC
Sports and Arts	– Turf, Travellers + Yacht clubs –	The Arts Club 1906 Many SCG members of the Royal Irish Yacht Club
Social	– Marlborough – (Prince of Wales' cronies)	Catholic Commercial Club

The reasons for this male social phenomenon would include the facts that:

Boarding schools and the services trained the upper classes to do without female society;

The Victorian wife was a dull, under-educated companion. This was the golden age of male friendships.

Smoking was not tolerated in the house. Indeed the snuff-takers ruled the clubs until the 1850s.

The upper classes valued personal privacy and shunned newsmen.

Those pre-Victorian clubs were informal meeting places in coffee houses or inns where gentlemen of like mind gathered together for some particular form of business or recreation. The extreme privacy of the select club-house was a Victorian development. It would seem likely that economic necessity must change this strict elitism.

The rules of the early clubs were simple documents. The code of behaviour was, no doubt, lenient but it was strongly influenced by the mess conventions built up by the important British regiments. Thus the controversial relaxing of restrictions in club-houses followed the increased indulgence in cigarettes by officers returned from the Crimean War. It was mess convention, not club bye-laws, which forbade certain topics of conversation: Religion; Politics – surely our Liberal/ Repealers did not observe any such inhibition! – and ladies by name. For similar reasons strangers were discouraged – in sharp contrast to modern club policies. It was only in 1916 that some degree of reciprocity was allowed for other clubs.

Gambling was a continuous pastime amongst the idle landowners in the 18th century Coffee House Clubs such as Daly's and, it must be said, Lloyd's of London. This craze spread to the middle classes as they became more wealthy after 1800. The 'betting books' were a feature in the private clubhouses and preserve, pickled in alcohol, the sporting wagers of Victorian gentlemen. Rulebooks distinguish between members playing cards for stakemoney and gambling by machines etc.

THE REFORM CLUB, LONDON

This club on the Pall Mall had much in common with the Stephen's Green Club. Founded by Edward Ellice M.P., it provided a home from home for those who favoured the swing of parliamentary power away from the land owners to the newly wealthy middle classes.

The Liberals, supported by O'Connell, were much in power during the twenty years from 1830. Hence the first committee in 1836 included Daniel O'Connell M.P.; The O'Connor (sic) Don M.P. and Barry O'Meara M.P. The future Lord Lieutenants Mulgrave and Ebrington were also officers.

The portraits and bust of O'Connell still grace the Reform Club to mark this shared history. The full length portrait by Joseph Haverty of O'Connell with his dog hangs most prominently in the entrance hall. There also is a copy of the 1846 bust by Edward Jones; the original being in the National Gallery of Ireland. However, the Pall Mall archives do not really disclose any contemporary references to The Stephen's Green Club. The Reform Club no longer has any political affiliations. However, *The Economist* sponsored a luncheon for members of the House of Commons at the Reform Club to commemorate the centenary of that great Liberal, John Bright M.P., who was so deeply concerned about Ireland. Their famous Chef, Alexis Soyer, was invited over to set up a famine relief soup kitchen. The suspicious Dubliners hunted him off back to his eponymous cutlets on the Mall!

There was an *Irish Reform Club* which presumably catered for the Liberals who were less radical in their anti-Unionism than O'Connell's followers. The Irish Reform Club rented No. 19 Dawson Street – now the Royal Irish Academy – from Gresham, the hotel-keeper, between 1845 and 1851.

A quirk of history has linked the Reform Club with the property redevelopment consortium for Dublin's Custom House Docks. Three prominent Liberal M.P..s were members of the Club: Richard Cobden, 1837–1856; Sir John Walmsley, 1837–1864 and William A. Wilkinson, 1836–1865. These ingenious Parliamentarians discovered a loophole in the unjust property franchise which effectively restricted voting power to the landed gentry. In 1856 they formed the British Land Company whose shareholders were thus qualified to vote in support of Gladstone's contentious Home Rule Bill. Now British Land plc is a member of that re-development consortium with Hardwicke and McInerney Properties.

The *Ulster Reform Club* was established in 1880 to cater for Liberal supporters but Gladstone's Home Rule Bill split the party. Indeed Charles Brett, one of the founders, was excluded from membership within the first year because he supported Gladstone's Home Rule policy against the 'Liberal Unionists' led by Lieut-Col. Frederick Crawford (1861–1952). After 1905 the club was affiliated to the Ulster Unionist Council. Be that as it may, the Ulster Reform Club members welcome visitors from Stephen's Green to their fine clubhouse at No. 4 Royal Avenue.

OTHER IRISH CLUBS

The social needs of Irish gentlemen have been catered for by their clubhouses which were, as Samuel Johnson remarked; 'places where people with common prejudices meet'

		Formation
I	Friendly Brothers	c. 1610
II	Masonic Order	1725
III	Hellfire Club	c. 1735
	Down Hunt Club (claims to be the oldest dining club in Ireland)	1751
IV	Kildare Street/University Club	1782
V	The Law Club of Ireland	1791
VI	Limerick Club	1813
VII	Cork and County Club	1823
VIII	Hibernian United Services Club (have produced an excellent *Historical Note 1832–1982* by the late John Donovan)	1832
IX	Ulster Reform (*see above*)	1880
X	Royal Irish Automobile Club	1901
XI	United Arts (have published a history for their first fifty years)	1907

I THE FRIENDLY BROTHERS – CIRCA 1610

The Friendly Brothers at Number 22 St. Stephen's Green included O'Connell amongst their members. Since its primary object was to put down duelling, the Brothers may claim to be *the* wholly successful club on the Green. It is not surprising that Daniel O'Connell was also a member there. His duel with D'Esterre was a traumatic incident in a career dedicated to non-violence. It was not uncommon for Stephen's Green and other clubs' members to join the Friendly Brothers because it was non-political.

An elegant research by Victor Jackson shows that the Ancient and Most Benevolent Order of the Friendly Brothers of St. Patrick was founded about 1610 in Galway of the 'Tribes'. These wealthy merchant families encouraged close friendship and the social virtues. Hence their object of the abolition of 'the barbarous practice of duelling'.

In 1750 the General Grand Knot of this already Ancient Order decided to move to Dublin. It flourished despite having no clubhouse of its own until it purchased Sackville (O'Connell) Street in 1820. The year 1886 saw the Order handsomely established at its present Georgian (1790) clubhouse.

At present there are nine Knots in Ireland and three in England.

II FREEMASONS OF IRELAND

The Masons came to Dublin in 1725 and were a dining club of roistering good fellows with a liberal outlook on the world around them. Many Catholics such as Daniel O'Connell were members. For so ancient a society the Masons have shown a remarkable resilience to adapt to changing times. However, their reputation for goodfellowship and benevolence is still clouded by a controversial public image of undesirable influence in Great Britain and elsewhere.

The Molesworth Hall is a most unusual clubhouse and well repays a visit. It was built in 1866 with fantastically rich mixtures of styles appropriate to the traditions of the Lodges. It is an interesting comparison with the magnificent Georgian clubhouse occupied by the Knights of St. Columbanus (1915) at number 8 Ely Place.

III HELLFIRE CLUB (CIRCA 1735)

That solid structure on Montpelier Hill is said to be the Speaker Tom Connolly's hunting lodge. Despite tradition it seems an unlikely venue for Black Masses, devil worship and suchlike contemporary pastimes. The satanic members of that infamously evil Hellfire club met in taverns such as The Eagle on Cork Hill and other hostelries around Dame Street. Laurence Parsons, Earl of Rosse, was a founder member.

IV KILDARE STREET CLUB (1782). INCLUDES 'SACKVILLE STREET' FROM 1923; UNIVERSITY CLUB (1850). MERGED 1976.

The Conservative landowners and their friends split off from the deep drinking and gambling of Daly's Club (1744–1823). Their Kildare Street society must have seemed an impregnable bastion against changes such as the reform of the franchise, the Land Acts and the whole industrial revolution. However, the balance of power moved in favour of the new wealth of the mainly Roman Catholic merchants and professional men.

The Kildare Street Club would then have been recognised as Ireland's premier club. Its rules and customs provided guide lines for behaviour in the many clubs formed during the nineteenth century. The history by Raymond F. Brooke provides a useful base for a more in-depth study of its immense social influence. So powerful were the political clubs such as Carlton and the Reform that Edward Ellice M.P. could describe Parliament as 'Club Government'.

Great poet but political Silly Billy – William Butler Yeats resigned from The Stephen's Green Club to join the Kildare Street, in disgust at the burning of great houses by the anti-Treaty 'Irregulars'.

The Sackville Street Club (1794–1923) catered for an extreme ascendancy group of Unionists. When it collapsed into the Kildare Street Club, The Stephen's Green Club purchased its luncheon hut at Punchestown.

There must have been little good fellowship with their neighbours the Catholic Commercial Club at 42 O'Connell Street.

After the closure of the hard-line Sackville Street Club even the largely Church of Ireland Unionist members of the Kildare Street Club had to take a realistic view of their future. The Irish Free State was a political fact which had to be accommodated. After 1923 many whose families had been associated with the Stephen's Green Club were elected to the Kildare Street Club, e.g.: Esmonde, Sir Anthony; Nugent, Sir Walter; Plunkett, Sir Horace; Yeats, William B.

Stephen's Green remained as the home place for the largely pro-treaty majority.

V THE LAW CLUB OF IRELAND (1791–1899)

The solicitors felt oppressed by the Benchers of The King's Inns and formed the Law Club which was the precursor of The Incorporated Law Society of Ireland (Charter 1852). By 1841 there were one hundred members elected by ballot with a clubhouse at 13 Dame Street. The official functions were taken over by the Law Society leaving the club to carry on its social objectives until it expired circa 1899. Its records are lost.

An echo of the Law Club is to be found in the stained glass panel preserved in the sociable clubroom at 'The Blew Coat Boys Hospital of King Charles II' in Blackhall Place. Its history is more appropriate to the development of the professions in Ireland than to the growth of clubs for the gentlemen of Dublin.

VI PROVINCIAL CLUBS

London-style clubs were established in all the principal towns in Ireland. Few survive.

The *Limerick Club* of 1813 claimed to be the first. It was established for the county gentlemen and was planned very closely on the Kildare Street pattern. Both Liberal and Tory Members of Parliament were members but all were Unionist. The city merchants had their own coffeeroom in the Commercial Building.

In the first half century smoking was restricted to the Taproom. The snufftakers objected to Turkish cigarettes and 'Beyroot pipe' smoke. It was only after the troops returned from the Crimea in 1856 that the Officers persuaded the Committee to permit more comfortable smoking rooms. Port and claret from the club cellars were to be had at three shillings and six pence per bottle. Champagne which increased in popularity in Ireland until 1914 was priced at 'seven and six'. On the other hand a pack of playing cards cost about five shillings – because of the heavy duty until the 1850s.

VII THE CORK CARD CASE

This was a *cause célèbre* in which the privacy of Cork's Unionist Club (formed in 1823) was exposed for the enjoyment of the public.

'A quiet round game'. Drawing from *Truth*, Christmas number 1891. The figure second from the right, back row, is King Edward VII. *(See 'Cork Card Case', p.49)*

Joseph Pike DL., was accused of cheating at cards. Following the unfortunate precedent of the Tranby Croft scandal involving Prince Edward, an attempt was made to hush up the incident. However, R.P. Beamish DL., as Trustee, decided that the allegation should be investigated. Pike took a libel action. On 23 May 1894, the Dublin jury found in his favour.

The atmosphere of contemporary society is perfectly described in *Twilight of the Ascendancy* by Mark Bence-Jones.

VIII THE ROYAL IRISH AUTOMOBILE CLUB

Two adjoining clubhouses demonstrate the metamorphosis of Irish society during Victoria's reign. In 1840 a pre-industrial economy survived. By 1901 the (Royal) Irish Automobile Club's formation recognised the advent of technology as a separate cultural development.

The (Royal) Irish Automobile Club held its first meeting in January 1901 as Queen Victoria lay dying. The Dawson Street 'motor house' was formally opened by the Liberal Viceroy, H.E. The Earl of Aberdeen and Ishobel, but few indentifiable Stephen's Green Club Members attended. The Members who attended were Walter Sexton, Dr. Alfred Smith, Dr. Donelan, (Sir) Thomas Talbot Power, Vice-Chairman. The latter officiated in the absence in London of Sir Horace Plunkett, President.

Aberdeen prophetically observed that "there is an obvious advantage in having a safe and central place where motorists can deposit their cars . . . it may, indeed, be regarded as a necessity."

The United Services Club racket court was leased to (R) I.A.C. in 1908. The communicating door at rear 'no. 9' has been sealed off.

MISCELLANEA

There were sevaral *Bankers* connected with the early Club:.

Guinness & Darley of Kildare Street – beside the club there – were 'Treasurers' to the Union Club in 1837–1839. This is an interesting history.

The Guinness family were strongly Conservative. Two scions thereof commenced business as Land Agents and Bankers about 1819. This partnership between Rundell Guinness and his younger brother Richard S. Guinness continued under the style of 'R.S. Guinness & Co.' until 1836. Rundell, who was a shrewd businessman, became concerned about Richard's spendthrift ways. Rundell withdrew from the partnership in 1836. He went on to form the well-known and successful Merchant Bank and Agency in College Green with John Ross Mahon of Castlegar, Co. Galway. Richard continued his agency and banking business in Kildare Street until the firm stopped payments and was wound up in 1848. Nothing daunted, he went on to a political career in the House of Commons.

I cannot confirm which Darley was associated with the ill-fated 'Guinness & Darley'. Perhaps it was Henry B. Darley who was on the Union Club Committee 1837–1839. The Darleys and the Guinness

Dawson Street, Dublin, showing the rear entrance of the Club and the RIAC *(Shaw's Guide)*

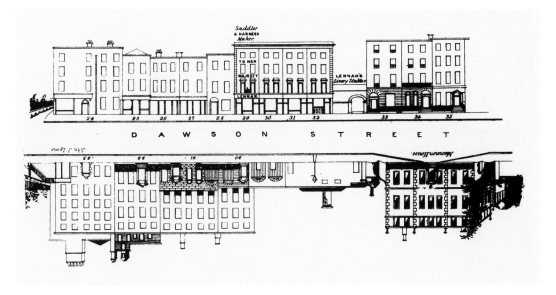

51

families inter-married. Rundell had served his time at the Darley Brewery alongside the Lepers' Stream in Stillorgan.

There were various Darleys named 'Henry' active in Dublin circa 1840. Henry Brewster Warren Darley, Barrister, had an office at No. 2 Kildare Street near the banking partnership of Guinness & Darley. He resided at 34 Merrion Square. I have not researched further to ascertain how Henry B. Darley fared financially as a result of this partnership and its subsequent failure in 1848 but those were the days of umlimited liability and spectacular crashes. (See below)

It is reasonable to suppose that the Stephen's Green Club appointed some other banker in 1840. Daniel O'Connell supported the formation of the Hibernian Bank (1825) and also of the National Bank of Ireland in London (1834). Dan would find it strange that his two 'Catholic' Banks should be taken over by the 'Church of Ireland' Bank of Ireland whose establishment power he disliked.

The Tipperary Bank. 'Tis a rare family that does not have a skeleton in the cupboard! John Sadlier (1814–1856), lawyer, politician and swindler, acted as Solicitor to the Stephen's Green Club in obtaining the Letter Patent of 1840. His subsequent banking career certainly did 'let the side down'.

Born at Shronhill, near Tipperary. Educated at Clongowes Wood College, Co. Kildare. He succeeded his uncle in a prosperous solicitor's practice in Dublin, but left the legal profession in 1846 to devote himself to his business interests. He became a director of the *Tippe-*

Soot and Sorrow: Smug Georgian fireplaces echo with the smothered cries of the 'climbing boys' who were forced up to sweep the chimneys. A Committee reported on the cruel health consequences, including cancer of the scrotum, but regulations were obstructed until 1875. No doubt the common Irish practice of pulling a live goose up through the chimney was also used. In 1815 one sweep was publically flogged at City Hall for maltreating his infant assistants. Audience pressure was so great that nine spectators were killed.

rary Joint-Stock Bank, which had been established about 1827 by his brother, and of a number of railway companies in England, France and Switzerland. Elected M.P. for Carlow 1847, he later sat for Sligo, and became one of the leaders of the group known as 'the Pope's Brass Band'. A junior lord of the Treasury, 1843–1853.

In 1856 he had overdrawn his account at the Tipperary bank by £200,000, and when a London bank refused to honour drafts on Tipperary, he committed suicide, his dead body being found on Hampstead Heath on 17th February 1856. It was discovered that the Tipperary bank was hopelessly insolvent, and depositors and others, mainly small farmers and clerks in the south of Ireland, lost about £400,000. To raise funds he had also forged land conveyances and railway share certificates. These relevations created a sensation. Dickens based the character of Mr. Merdle in *Little Dorrit* on Sadlier.

Did Sadlier, in fact, commit suicide on that wintry Hampstead Heath by drinking 'Essential Oil of Bitter Almonds?' Many believed that he escaped to some safer country just as his brother James had done.

John Sadlier (*Illustrated London News*). (See 'Tipperary Bank, p.52)

Peter La Touche (1723–1828) was a successful Huguenot merchant banker who resided at no. 15 St. Stephen's Green as well as at Bellevue, Delgany, his remarkably landscaped gardens, and at Lugalla, Co. Wicklow. In 1812, after the death of Parsons, Earl of Rosse, no. 9 (then numbered 10) passed into Peter's hands – presumably as a result of a financing transaction. The La Touche banking partnership had a preference for aristocratic mortgages in the St. Stephen's Green area.

Peter was very charitable – like his father David II of whom it is said that he walked abroad, his pockets full of shillings for the poor. If reproached for indiscriminate giving he would reply "Si mon shilling tombe à propos une fois sur dix c'est assez' On the other hand, they were bigoted opponents of Catholic Emancipation.

Four of the family were members of the Irish parliament who voted against the Union in 1800. No doubt they could perceive the disastrous fall in Dublin property values, which did not recover until after the Famine.

With his two brothers David and John, Peter served as a founding director of the Bank of Ireland in 1783. The family were promoters of the Kildare Street Club in 1782 and served as its 'Treasurers'. Peter La Touche died without issue. Indeed it is strange that the La Touche name, which was so strong a century ago, has completely died out.

* * *

Duelling is a fascinating custom but this bloody chapter in Irish history was ending by 1827. The last recorded Irish duel took place in 1838 between O'Hara and Finn on the North Bull, Portmarnock.

However, Norman Leslie of Glaslough fought a sword duel in Egypt as late as 1910.

Single combat as an honourable method of resolving quarrels between gentle folk ceased in England also but continued in France, Germany and America. Some say duelling ceased because Queen Victoria disapproved of her officers shooting each other. Perhaps another factor was the lecture at the Royal Dublin Society in 1838 by the famous Dublin gunsmith, Rigby. He demonstrated the accuracy and killing power of his modern pistols.

Every schoolboy knows that Daniel O'Connell killed his political opponent Alderman D'Esterre on the Hill of Allen in 1815. Others claim Lyon's Hill (U.C.D. Faculty of Agriculture) as the site. The rough-tongued O'Connell was plagued by antagonists wanting his blood. In his stead Morgan fought against Lieut. Col. Lord Alvaney in 1835. Two shots were exchanged at the Chalk Farm duel but no one was hurt. However, the O'Connells declined Disraeli's challenge in the same year. Likewise he refused a challenge to a duel which was issued by the American ambassador. This arose because of 'The Liberator's' denunciation of both George Washington and of the ambassador as slave owners.

Another O'Connell – no relation – known as 'Lord Kilmallock' offered to fight all and sundry who sought satisfaction from the Liberator.

The lowly folk art of faction fighting continued its deadly saga until the 1880s. Litigation was taking over from armed combat – much to the benefit of the many lawyers who were members of the Club.

* * *

GALLOWS ON THE GREEN

Harman's mansion was an excellent vantage point for the popular recreation of viewing the public executions which were carried out on the Green. There seem to have been two gallows – one on the Merrion Row end of Beaux' Walk, the other at the Harcourt Street corner. It would be interesting to know when the last capital punishment took place on the Green.

The new gaols were built at Kilmainham, Richmond and Mountjoy in early Victorian times: the Irish design included a permanent gallows over the front entrance. This labour-saving apparatus removed the tumultuous spectacles on the open Green which were so celebrated in street ballads.

Some notorious executions were:-

1640   Atherton, Bishop of Waterford, executed for bestiality

The execution of Bishop
Atherton, 1640
(National Library)

before an immense crowd on the Green.

1764   Darky Kelly, brothel keeper, was burned to death on the Green.

1798   Shelbourne House was a ghastly torturing barrack for suspected rebels.

1815   The last public whipping took place at City Hall (Royal Exchange). Nine spectators were crushed to death in this early example of ineffective crowd control.

1867–8   The last public execution in Britain took place. The 'bold Fenian Men' were hanged outside Newgate Prison.

LEISURE PURSUITS OF CLUB MEMBERS CIRCA 1840

Backgammon and chess – together with whist and billiards – were the great pastimes of Victorian gentlemen. The renewals of backgammon boxes and chess boards are recorded in early minutes. Indeed the Hibernian United Services Club appreciated this need when their founding committee invested in their equipment in 1832. However, the gallant officers probably had more 'time to kill' than the average Stephen's Green Club member. Backgammon, with its blend of dice and skill, did make a short comeback after World War II. Sir Horace Plunkett and his friends played chess but the rattle of chessmen onto the board has not been heard in the Club within living memory.

The rule prohibiting 'games of hazard or mere chance' has a long tradition. The 'one-armed bandits' have forced their way into some foreign clubs but do not fit into the Dublin social tradition.

The Racket Court was built by the United Services Club in 1846 and was leased by them to the (R) I.A.C. in 1908. The early minutes and rules of The Stephen's Green Club mention racket playing. There is still a doorway from the courtyard into the R.I.A.C. garage. The old rules stipulated that there should be two locks – one controlled by each club.

FASHIONABLE DRESS CIRCA 1840

How did the original members of the Club dress in pre-famine Dublin? The answer to this question can be found in Mairead Dunlevy's classic *Dress in Ireland*. Clearly a city gentleman's clothes were of great social significance. There was quite a rigid code which was largely based on London styles and the viceregal court dress. In addition there was a wide range of garments to be worn when travelling by carriage or for

Advertisment for John G. McGee, 1846 *(Dress in Ireland)*. Fashionable dress when the Club was formed.

PANTECHNETHECA
TAILORING,
WOOLLEN DRAPERY, READY-MADE CLOTHING,
AND
LONDON HAT
Warehouse,
46 and 48, High-street,
BELFAST.

JOHN G. M'GEE & CO.
PROPRIETORS.

The Proprietors respectfully announce, that the above Establishment is now Re-opened, after a close of two months; during which time very extensive alterations and improvements have been made, rendering it now one of the most spacious and splendid places of business in the North of Ireland.

BESPOKE DEPARTMENT.

The entire of the first floor has been fitted up and set apart exclusively to this department. The STOCK consists of every shade and quality of

Superfine West of England Cloths, Cassimeres, French Velvet and Satin Vestings, &c.

Which are made to measure in the first style of fashion, and an elegant fit always guaranteed, being conducted by two Foremen Cutters from the West End of London.

Scale of Prices.

	First Quality.	Medium.	Second Quality.
	£ s. d.	£ s. d.	£ s. d.
Dress Coats, any colour	2 18 0	2 8 8	1 16 0
Frock Coat, any colour	3 8 0	2 18 0	2 5 0
Riding Coat, any colour	3 0 0	2 10 0	1 18 0
Black Dress Trousers	1 8 0	1 4 0	1 1 0
Coloured Trousers	1 6 0	1 3 0	0 18 0
Waistcoats	0 14 0	0 12 6	0 8 6

Contracts by the Year.

	First Quality.	Medium.	Second Quality.
Two Suits in the Year	8 4 0	6 15 0	5 10 0
Three Suits in the Year	12 0 0	9 15 0	8 10 0
Four Suits in the Year	15 12 0	12 12 0	10 10 0

Each Suit to be returned on receipt of its successor. Gentlemen contracting for three or more Suits are allowed Two Suits in wear during the whole term.

the traditional outdoor sports of hunting, fishing and shooting.

Ms. Dunlevy suggests a comprehensive wardrobe for the fashion-conscious clubman circa 1840:-

Coats	– Four Morning Coats
	– One Fitted Frock Coat
	– One Dress Coat
	(The 'smoking jacket' was a mid-Victorian requirement.)
	The 'Travelling Ulster' from John McGee of Belfast was widely worn. The Mackintosh was practical for Irish weather but had an offensive stench.
Waistcoats	were colourful and splendid. It is hoped that these O'Connellites adhered to their principles by buying the Irish made materials such as poplin.

Advertisement for Benjamin Hyam, who in 1851 succeeded Moses & Co. at 30 Dame Street, Dublin. *(Mairead Dunleavy: Dress in Ireland).* Club servants would have been dressed in these styles.

Trousers	– Six Morning Trousers with colours contrasting with the coat. The fly would still have been fall fronted. One Evening Breeches.
Shirts	– Handmade of Irish linen – probably white, with standing collar.
Cravat or stock	
Shoes	– indoor 'slippers' with pumps for full dress. The streets were filthy so spats and gaiters were a practical addition. The granite setts remained on the Green until 1925. However, the 'Wellington' boots were more likely to be found around the corner in Kildare Street.
Hats	– The silk top hat not yet been superseded by the bowler hat. Indeed Drummond's Dublin Metropolitan Policemen wore silk hats and Beaver Row and Mespil Road were still the centres for numerous hat manufacturers.
Golden accessories	were much in evidence. The watch, sovereign case and chain were *de rigueur*. Rings and cuff links were necessary. The cane had replaced the sword.
Wigs	had gone out of fashion except in the law courts but a wide variety of hairstyles and beards were in evidence.

The merchant tailor system provided an efficient local service. Advertisements offered annual contracts for gentlemen's clothing. A cost of less than £50 a year is suggested but would be based on the 'sweat shop' wages prevalent in Dublin at that time.

Dublin was still a home for cheap hand tailoring and such-like cottage industry. However, the bespoke factory was coming and would sound a death knell for locally made materials, hats and accessories. O'Connell's '42 Club' did perceive the need to try to preserve Irish manufacturers but this was in conflict with his vigorously free-trade politics.

The numerous club servants would have worn special livery appropriate to their function. The necessity of a personal valet is recognised in early club rules.

The contemporary lady folk of these clubmen were already restricted by the beautiful but overly genteel fashion of the Victorian age.

After the Famine, Dublin slowly came back to life. 1853 saw the Industrial Exhibition on Leinster Lawn organised and partly paid for by William Dargan. Walter Sweetman served on the Committee. For the first time in Dublin there was a representative selection of the fine arts available to the public. The interest thus generated sparked off the National Gallery of Ireland.

David R. Pigot and his Solicitor son John, with Maziere Brady and Walter Berwick were the prime movers.

The RT. Hon. Alexander Macdonnell was also active on the Committee. Others who served in some capacity included:-

Thomas Hutton	B.L.
F. French	M.P.
P. McCann	M.P.
W.H.F. Cogan	M.P.
Francis P. Codd	
John O'Connell	
Patrick Sweetman	
Thomas O'Hagan	
Sir Colman Michael O'Loghlin	
James Henry Monahan (father of H.J.)	
Alderman Denis Moylan	

THE END OF OUR BEGINNING

The first 35 years of our Club's history was a time when convulsive forces changed society and the economy. By 1875 the Club was fixed in an increasingly self-confident groove which brought it through to the post 1922 era.

Our dignified Clubhouse was essentially a private place where gentlemen of liberal mind could socialise isolated from the clamours of home and market place.

The past has been faithfully chronicled – the future is there for us to guide as new ways replace the old rituals:

Et antiquum documentum
Novo cedat ritui

The Paintings and Sculpture

CIARAN MACGONIGAL

Ciaran MacGonigal

Like all clubs ours is no exception in that it has a number of works which are of more immediate interest to the Members than to a strict accounting in the history of art. That being said however, the paintings in the Club give a flavour of a period in its history when the practice of commissioning artists to paint portraits or to carve portrait busts was a regular occurrence.

The indices of many an art historical reference book are packed with references noting that the Club resolved to present a portrait of Mr. (or Sir or Lord) so and so, and the portrait to be commissioned from such and such an artist. The fact that several Presidents of the Royal Hibernian Academy of Art lived near the Club may have influenced the Members to commission artists such as Sir Thomas Jones or Stephen Catterson Smith, both PRHAs, to paint presentation portraits to those whom the Club wished to honour. In addition at one time the Earl Spencer, a Viceroy, and The Earl of Bessborough who lived in Piltown Co. Kilkenny, seemed to have a considerable influence upon the taste in art of the Club, as numbers of portrait commissions via the Club seemed to have come through their influence and patronage. The link of artists with the Club was lessened by the establishment of the Arts Club in the early years of the 20th century, and the last specific link with the RHA was in the person of Leo Whelan, who gave the works of art in the back bar. I can remember meeting Leo Whelan as he moved from or to a Club lunch and his studio in Lower Baggot Street, and on racing days, to which he was addicted, he and Madam Margaret Bourke Sheridan (The Irish Diva) would move in an ever more stately fashion along the Green.

Many of those works which were commissioned for the Club have not survived the passage of time, so that those remaining are all the more important as a glimpse in the patterns of patronage of the arts exercised in earlier days by our Members.

Portrait Bust of Daniel O'Connell:

Carved in 1846, this is a very good example of representational sculpture in the 19th century. Here the sitter is shown as the man of action, resting for a moment, his travelling cloak thrown over his shoulder. The ideal in this type of iconography is to indicate the sitter as a popular Tribune of the people; a harking back to ancient Greece and Rome.

This portrait bust was exhibited in 1846 at the Royal Academy, and had been carved from a plaster version which exists in The Reform Club, London. It is the work of the Dublin sculptor John Edward Jones (1806–1862).

Daniel O'Connell

Portrait Bust of Pierce Mahony:

This work is also by John Edward Jones and was exhibited at The Royal Academy of Arts, London, in 1846 and subsequently at The Royal Hibernian Academy of Arts, Lower Abbey Street, in 1853, number 454 – where the sitter is described as 'The late Pierce Mahony, DL.'

One of the reasons why work like this and the bust of Daniel O'Connell were displayed on plinths was that they were intended to be seen at night, by lamp or candle-light. In the 18th and 19th centuries almost all sculpture galleries were viewed by lamplight, the light being held or placed *behind* the work.

The sculptor, John Edward Jones was born in Dublin in 1806, the son of the painter Edward Jones. Initially he trained as an engineer under Alexander Nimmo. He lived in London but returned regularly to Dublin and exhibited at the RHA between 1847 and 1854. Most of his Dublin pieces had Irish connections or interest. Jones had an

Pierce Mahony

extensive sculpture practice and his capacity for achieving a dignified, yet lively image is well captured in these two works which are in the Club.

61

Sir Percy Nugent

Edward Fottrell

Portrait of Sir Percy Nugent:
This, with the portrait of his father-in-law, Walter Sweetman, was probably painted by Sir Thomas Jones, PRHA, who had already been commissioned by the Club to paint a portrait of WALTER SWEETMAN. The portraits are typical 'club' portraits of a fairly routine sort, yet give a good sense of the period and the difficulties which portrait painters encountered in the middle of the 19th century. The country was uneasy after the famine and there were no really heroic 'Irish' figures who could be used. In a sense, the iconography of portraiture in Ireland was in transition, and remained so until the very end of the century.

Sir Thomas Jones (1823–1839) was reared in unusual circumstances by the Archdale family at their house just around the corner from the Club in Kildare Place. Jones was a very popular and club-type painter: quite a number of his pictures were commissioned by The Stephen's Green Club, The Friendly Brothers, The Royal St. George and The United Services Club.

Edward Fottrell by Walter Osborne RHA (1859–1903):
Osborne, the son of William Osborne, RHA, is now one of the best known Irish painters; in his day he was a successful and popular figure in the Dublin Castle set. His landscapes and genre pictures were much admired, but he made his living from the painting of portraits. This portrait is typical of his male portraits, where the figure is painted in the manner of a Dutch portrait, with a reliance on cast shadow and a good deal of chiaroscuro. Osborne had a considerable capacity for rendering a likeness and, without over-flattering his sitters, generally pleased them.

Walter Sweetman

Leo Whelan RHA 1892–1956
(1937)
Born in Dublin, he studied at the
Metropolitan School of Art under
Orpen. His works, which include
portraiture and genre paintings, are
much sought after today.

The artist had his studio in Lower
Baggot Street, and I can recall him
very clearly making his passage from
his studio via the Shelbourne to the
Club. Leo Whelan was also a great
racing man, and much of his later
painting practice revolved around
members of the Turf Club which at
that time was around the corner in
Hume Street; these places, and our
house in Ely Place, as well as Jammets
and on Thursday 'The Wicklow'
formed a large part of his later life.

Leo Whelan

63

The Ward Hunt

Engraving of the Ward Hunt, with Earl Spencer

The engraving is taken from a painting by William Osborne RHA., (1823–1901)

Osborne was a painter of animals and hunting scenes. Many of his paintings around the late 1870s were of the Ward Union Hunt, and those who hunted with it and hunted the pack. This painting, or rather the painting from which the print is derived, was exhibited in Dublin in 1880, and was popular enough to be engraved; the engravings presumably were sold to the members of the Hunt, and those who followed Stag packs.

Also in 1880, in the RHA, Osborne exhibited a portrait of Charles Brindley, Huntsman of the Ward Union Hounds, who likewise appears in this print.

Osborne was the father of Walter Osborne RHA.

Suite of 16 Architectural Prints by Giovanni Battista Piranesi (1720–1778)

Piranesi was a well known Venetian-born etcher, architect and archaeologist. He maintained the superiority of Etruscan or Roman architecture over that of Greece. His etchings of the views of Rome known as 'Vedute' were very popular and formed most people's imagination as to what Rome was like. These appear to be part of an original 18th century suite of works which came into the Club at some date unknown. These works are much collected and valued today.

SPY cartoons

Members' Bar

These cartoons which range over an important period of Irish life from

Captain Boycott of 1881, to Tim Healy, who became our first Governer-General and taking in along the way Lord Ardilaun (Guinness) who gave Stephen's Green to Dublin's citizens; Lord Iveagh, The Irish Sarjeant, Lord Hemphill (SGC 1859), Lord Dunraven and George Wyndham (of the land acts) Fred Archer the jockey, John Dillon and Lord Morris (an ancestor of one of our Members), John Redmond and George Moore.

One is reminded of the passing parade of power in late 19th and early 20th century Ireland in these much sought after cartoons.

Engraving of the Royal Visit to Punchestown, 1870

This engraving, published by Cranfield, is a typical 19th century production showing groups of figures arranged according to the iconography of the age, when the main figures are isolated by the use of a lighter half tone to make them appear dressed in white. It predates naturally enough the popular use of photography, and was much patronised by the masses as well as by the middle classes. Frequently, all that remains of well known paintings are the engravings of the period.

Nude Study, line and wash; three etchings

Sir William Orpen

These works were given to the Club by one of our members, the late Leo Whelan RHA. Orpen (1878–1931) is one of our more famous artists today, and his work is much collected and avidly sought after in sales and auctions. He was the subject of the major biography by Bruce Arnold *Mirror to an Age*, published 1981. This biography helped to resuscitate his reputation as a painter.

Orpen taught in the Metropolitan School of Art, Dublin, and was one of the most important influences on early 20th century Irish art and its development. He was a member of the RHA in Dublin and the RA in London. His works are to be found in major collections in Ireland, the UK and the US.

Nude, by William Orpen

65

Rumours of Wars: 1875-1922

BERNARD SHARE

Bernard Share

On 2 February 1875 the House Committee, under the Hon. C. Trench – in public life Chairman of Dublin Quarter Sessions – agreed that the estimate of Maguire & Son for the installation of a speaking-tube from the landing on the stairs to the door of the bar room and from the kitchen to the top of the stairs should be accepted: the cost was £4 10s 6d. The following month it was decided to abandon the old water cistern and install a new one to connect with the Vartry pipe, which had reached Dublin from Wicklow in 1868. This major civic advance was the work of the railway pioneer William Dargan who, in the words of Oliver St. John Gogarty, 'led into Dublin the soft water from Wicklow's granite hills and made fountains for the town'. Estimates for new furniture and curtains from Messrs. McDowell and Arnott were accepted and negotiations opened concerning railings – both with the United Services Club and with the Corporation – to extend the area two feet towards the street. The latter agreed to settle for one.

In February John Mitchel returned from the USA, having been elected in absentia as MP for Co. Tipperary. He died in March, a month before Charles Stewart Parnell entered Parliament for Meath. On 29 June an International rifle match was held in Dublin between Ireland and America – the Americans won – and the visiting team was invited to make use of the Club during their stay. On 6 August the Exhibition Palace echoed to the strains of Professor Glover's National Oratorio, 'St Patrick of Tara', performed by a chorus of 500 with orchestra, in celebration of the centenary of the birth of Daniel O'Connell. In September there were storms across the whole country, with serious flooding.

The 1876 edition of Charles Eason's *Almanac and Hand-book for Ireland* carried an advertisement by Fred. Lewis & Co. of 6, Fleet Street, confidently assuring prospective customers that his Electric Oil would 'make Hair and Whiskers grow where they never previously grew'. By 1892, when Club records are again available after a hiatus of 16 years, fashions have changed and the General Committee is resolving 'that the men servants be required to shave their upper lip'. On 5 November Gibney and Fulham, waiters who had omitted to conform to the requirement, were noticed to leave. The following year – too late – alas, in their case – the *Evening Herald* reported the publication of a book 'on shaving and how to do it'.

Those passing years had witnessed changes in the world beyond the extended railings somewhat more fundamental than the eclipse of the fashion for the hirsute. In 1880 St. Stephen's Green had been opened to the public through the beneficence of Lord Ardilaun; in the same year that one of the Club's early protagonists, Daniel O'Connell, was again in the news. 'In common with most of my fellow citizens'. wrote "Art Lover" to the editor of the *Evening Mail*, 'permit me to express my abhorrence of the basement [sic] for the O'Connell statue that has been laid at the northern end of the new bridge into Sackville Street'. The writer went on to recommend its removal to 'the classic gardens at the Rotunda or to the spacious and enclosed square at St. Stephen's Green'. Electric light came to the Dublin streets in 1881, and, minimally, to the Club in 1892, when, on 26 March, the Electrical Engineering Co. offered to fix four 100 candle-power lamps in the Smoking Room and four of 32 candle-power in the hall outside for £34 10s 6d. The estimate was accepted, even though the Committee had previously decided not to spend more than five guineas on the new-fangled idea. Dublin's first manual telephone exchange opened in December 1880 with five subscribers – it might have been simpler to employ a messenger – and it was not until 1894 that a suggestion from several Members that the Club should be linked to the system was adopted. This may have reflected a need to sustain sporting contacts (the Irish Rugby Football Union had been founded in 1880, the city's first golf club, the Royal Dublin, in 1885, Fitzwilliam Tennis Club in 1877, and *McCall's Racing Guide* ordered in 1892 for the Smoking Room) or, perhaps, to keep abreast of the rising political ferment in the world outside.

The foundation of the Land League in 1879 had linked the movement for agrarian reform with that for political independence, creating a momentum that was to impinge upon the affairs of the country for the course of the period under review. Charles Stewart Parnell was given the freedom of the City of Dublin in 1882, the year of the Phoenix Park Murders of Chief Secretary Cavendish and Under-Secretary Burke. The following year William Redmond, (Home Rule), defeated The O'Conor Don (Liberal) (1907) in the by-election in Wexford town. In 1906 the sympathy of the Committee was to be

67

Charles Owen, the
O'Conor Don

extended to the family of the latter 'who was for 37 years one of the most honoured and esteemed members of the Club'. Political life continued to reflect the divergent positions of those whose ideal was founded on that of 'a nation once again' and those who adhered to the status quo. The first Home Rule Bill was introduced to the British House of Commons in 1886. The previous year Dublin Corporation had voted 41 to 17 against taking part in the official welcome for the visiting Prince of Wales; but in 1897, when riots in the city marked the Diamond Jubilee of Queen Victoria, the Club spent £26 10s 8d on 'illuminations'. 1890 saw the trauma and bitterness of the Parnell split, and the death, in the following year, of the man whom many still venerated as 'the Uncrowned King of Ireland'.

Little of all this, understandably, was reflected in the day to day pre-occupations of the Club: though its membership at the period could be said to represent most shades of opinion short of the most extreme. The Committee, as is customary, had its attention directed to the miniature drama of domestic affairs. The manager having absconded with plate and plated ware, the new incumbent, Mr Gavin, was obliged to sell shares to make good the deficit and complained that five members owed him money. The hall porter applied on 25 May 1892 to the Committee to reimburse him for postage and other items which he was paying out of his wages. Whether or not intended as a quid pro quo, the same porter was in 1893 awarded a suit of morning clothes. There were complaints about the cook and the cooking and, in November 1893, about the shortness of the Dinner on the Leopardstown nights. In December a set of chessmen and a chess board were provided and the size of the billiard balls adjusted to $2\frac{1}{16}$ inches. The following July it was reported that the bedroom porter, Joseph Brierton, had died of cancer; but 'the Committee did not see their way to subscribe towards a fund for his family'. In fairness it must be said that his illness had been a long one, during which he had been in regular receipt of his wages.

While chess, billiards and cards may have satisfied the more sedentary gentlemen, the range of established outdoor sports was rapidly expanding (the first soccer match at Dalymount was played in 1901, Bohs beating Shels 2-0) and golf, tennis, motoring and cycling were winning adherents among Club members. 'HOW TO ENJOY YOUR CYCLE DURING THE WINTER, ran an advertisement in the *Evening Herald* for 5 December 1893: 'Pop it at the Great Central Pawn Office, 48 Fleet Street, the only office in Dublin where Cycles are thoroughly understood and properly cared'. The new mode of locomotion caught on to the extent that in May 1897 the Committee was obliged to direct that 'a notice be put up in a prominent place requesting members not to leave cycles at the entrance but to make use of the new shed provided for the purpose in the front area'. Some few years later, in May 1905, they were being asked by the Secretary of the Kildare Street Club to give a silver cup for the inter-club servants'

The Cascade. St. Stephen's Green. *(Gallaher: 'Irish View Scenery' cigarette card series, 1910).*

THE CASCADE, STEPHEN'S GREEN, DUBLIN

69

Sir Horace Plunkett in his De Dion Bouton c1900: a pioneer motorist. *(Elizabeth, Countess of Fingall: 'Seventy Years Young').*

bicycle race. With the turn of the century, however, there were more serious events to occupy their deliberations – events which, though occurring on far foreign fields, were not without their local repercussions. The Second Boer War, which broke out in 1899, prompted a direction to the Secretary to order War Telegrams from Central News Ltd. A large pro-Boer demonstration was held at Beresford Place, Dublin on 1 October, a few days before hostilities commenced, but reports subsequently revealed that the war produced the highest ever number of Irish recruits for the regular army.

As the new century was ushered in a sub-committee was appointed to decorate the exterior of the Club in honour of the impending visit of Queen Victoria: the sum of £25 was allocated. The following week, however, on 21 March, it was agreed that something more elaborate would be required and the matter was referred to the General Committee. In April the old lady was enthusiastically received by Dubliners, in spite of nationalist protests, and knighted a local baker, Joseph Downes, thereafter popularly known as Lord Barmbrack. The following September telegrams were ordered from Exchange Telegraph Co. to keep members informed of the result of the general election, which resulted in Lord Salisbury retaining power and a Home Rule representation of 81 seats. Closer to home the foundation of the (later Royal) Automobile Club involved members Horace Plunkett (1918) and Walter Sexton (1918) and inaugurated a continuing era of con-

70

tiguity between the two clubs. In 1902 difficulties were reported in arranging for a new lease on the SGC's premises, Lady Milltown's solicitor indicating that she was insisting on an increase of £50 a year on the current rent, the new 500 year lease being conditional upon £1500 being spent on improvements. The General Committee considered the matter, the result of their deliberations being the closing of the Club during the summer for renovations, members availing of hospitality extended by the United Services and Ormond Clubs. The staff were not so well situated: all with two years' service and over, as well as the head porter, were retained, but others received notice to leave.

It is the nature of Club minutes to record such minutiae rather than the main issues preoccupying the nation: royal visits, political ferment, civil strife, surface only as taciturn committee resolutions or footnotes to the annual reports. The day to day details are, however, in their own way revealing both of the temper of the age and of the predilections of the membership; they are particularly revealing of the conditions attaching to the employment of the Club staff as reflecting the general relationships between employer and employee at the time. The billiard markers, for example, provide a case in point. In February 1903 it was agreed that one Rooney be allowed one night off a week, except for 'any occasions when his services could not be dispensed with without inconvenience'. Alas for Rooney, his services were summarily dispensed with the following week for 'drinking and going out

Coach at St Stephen's Green: Kitt Malcomson and Sir James Power.

71

without notice'. A successor, Joseph Greally, fared better, even though it was decided, in October 1907, that he not be given any holidays as he had been on sick leave for 12 weeks during the year. He was, however, awarded five shillings out of £1 he had found in the Club and which had remained unclaimed; and in July of the following year Judge Dodd intimated that he was considering appointing him as his tipstaff. One hopes, though it is not recorded, that Rooney took his cue and profited thereafter. The turnover of staff at the period was high: the Christmas List, 1904 showed only three employees with three years' service or more; and one of these and the longest serving, head housemaid Lottie Foster, left to be married in May 1905 after ten years with the Club, which awarded her £10 from the Christmas fund.

She had probably earned it. The visit of King Edward and Queen Alexandra in 1903, the seminal Bloomsday of June 1904 and the opening of the Abbey that December with Lady Gregory's *Spreading the News* were all overshadowed within the precincts – and the minutes – by the exigencies of a resident member, Count Frederick Leopold von Stolberg-Stolberg (1891) who, having presented a set of *The General Stud Book* to the Club in 1903, was granted in the following January permission to attach an Exerciser to the door of his bedroom on condition he be held responsible for any damage to Club property. To which side of the door the apparatus was affixed is not made clear. The year following, 1906, the Count was instrumental in causing the dismissal of the Hall Porter, McGowan, who, he said, had delayed in handing him a telegram. In 1909 the Count's concern was with unsatisfactory attendance at breakfast, in the wake of which the Committee, perhaps in self-defence, added him to their number. But to little avail. In January 1912 he was complaining that a letter written by him and placed in the Club post box had not been posted at the proper hour. Was it simple patriotism, one wonders, that promoted Mr Hickson, on 2 February 1916, to call attention to the fact that 'the name of Count Stolberg (an alien enemy) is retained on the list of members'? The matter was referred to the subsequent Annual General Meeting, which decided to take no action. The Count's last recorded manifestation was at the following year's Reading Out Dinner, when his name was amongst those in deficit and he was not answered for.

If Count Stolberg was largely an intramural phonemenon there were many members at the period who were playing – or destined to play – a more public role on a wider stage. In 1909 the newly-appointed Attorney General and Solicitor General, Redmond Barry and C.A. O'Connor both fell within this category and a fellow-member, Lane Joynt, suggested that a Club Dinner be given to honour the appointees. The decision of the Committee is interesting in the light of the Club's origin and orientation: 'that, having regard to the distinctively social

Saturday July 17th 1875

Present: Right Hon. McCogan Miss'' Sweetman, Blackall, Corbett Fitzgerald, Browne, Pigot, Murphy, Findlater

Resolved: Mr Greene's letter of the 17th ins' read —
That an extraordinary General Meeting be called for Tuesday the 3rd of August & accordingly That the following notice be posted —
A member having violated Rule 23 of the club and having thus incurred the penalty of expulsion in accordance with Rule 34 The Committee hereby summon an extraordinary General Meeting of the club for Tuesday next August the 3rd to investigate the charge brought against him

Resolved: That the estimate of £19. 0. 0 for a parcel room at the end of the new hall be accepted —

Resolved: That on a certificate of Mr Brown's a cheque for £300 shall be given to Mr Bolton on account of works

Resolved: That a speaking tube + bell in connection with

From the Club minute book, 1875

and non-political character of the Club and the fact that there would be a danger of party interpretation being placed on the proposed dinner, if given under official auspices, they could not sanction the proposal, while at the same time recognising the right of any member or individual members to entertain the Law Officers, or any other guests'. This is an important statement in the light of the growing polarisation of political opinion, both domestic and constitutional, as Ireland passed through the period of the 1913 Strike, the First World War conscription issue, the 1916 Rising and the Civil War. Whereas the echoes from the Boer Wars had been faint within the walls of No. 9 (though the view from the windows was to be embellished in 1904-7 by the erection of the Memorial Arch at the corner of St. Stephen's Green to those Dubliners who fell in the conflict: a monument known to those of nationalist opinion as 'Traitors' Gate'), the impact of these more immediate events was considerably wider. The Strike, which brought the city's tramway system to a halt and was the cause of great hardship, delayed the completion of building and construction work, according to the Report for the Year 1913. The effects of the conflict of 1914–18 were to alter the conditions of Irish life almost beyond recognition – though the Club, unlike its near neighbour in Kildare Street, was to suffer less traumatic change by the shifting of the political focus to Leinster House.

A bare fortnight after Britain declared war on Germany on 4 August a telegram was received from the Prince of Wales' National Relief Fund Committee asking the Committee and members to co-operate in the raising of monies for the purpose of alleviating distress caused by the outbreak of hostilities. On 29 October subscriptions amounting to £1032 were forwarded through the Lord Mayor of Dublin, the Committee then turning its attention to the implications of the Intoxicating Liquor (Temporary Restrictions) Act which, inter alia, would suspend in all registered clubs the supply or consumption of drink between 8 p.m. and 7 a.m. A resolution proposed by John McCann and seconded by T.L. Plunkett authorised the Secretary to 'take such steps as may be advised, either in cooperation with the Dublin clubs similarly circumstanced or separately to apply to the Rt. Hon. the Recorder to make an exception. . . in the case of the Stephen's Green Club on the grounds that such an order would constitute an interference with the convenience and general habits of the ordinary

YOUR KING and COUNTRY need another 100,000 MEN.

IN THE PRESENT grave national emergency another 100,000 men are needed at once to rally round the Flag and add to the ranks of our new Armies

Terms of Service

Extension of age limit. Height Reduced to Normal Standard.

Age on enlistment 19 to 38. Ex-soldiers up to 45. Minimum height 5ft. 3in.: chest 34½ins. Must be medically fit. General Service for the War.

Men enlisting for the duration of the War will be able to claim their discharge, with all convenient speed, at the conclusion of the War.

Pay at Army Rates

Married Men or Widowers with Children will be accepted and if at time of enlistment a recruit signs the necessary form. Separation Allowance under Army conditions is issuable at once to the Wife and in certain circumstances to other dependents. Pamphlet with full details from any Post Office

How to Join.

Men wishing to join should apply in person at

The RECRUITING DEPOT, 24 Great Brunswick St., Dublin

or at any Military Barrack or at any Recruiting Office. The address of the latter can be obtained from Post Offices or labour Exchanges.

GOD SAVE THE KING

and resident members. . . .' The stated purpose of the legislation was that of 'maintaining order and suppressing drunkenness' – objectives which, though the Committee believed them to be necessary in the public interest, were of no relevance where the Club was concerned: 'The freedom of the Club from the suggested restrictions', it suggested in a motion adopted on 2 November, 'could in no way lead to a continuance of the evils at which the suggested Order is aimed'. In consultation with the secretaries of other clubs Mr Fitzgibbon (not an SGC member) was briefed to appear before the Recorder – with satisfactory results.

Even before the exigencies of war began to make themselves felt, the Club had been reviewing its internal organisation and instigating a number of fundamental changes. The bye-laws were revised in 1907 and a deed executed vesting the Club property in new Trustees. New government legislation affecting clubs proposed in 1910 prompted the Committee to co-opt James Chambers, KC, MP (1900); and other members who were also MPs were communicated with. During the honorary secretaryship of H.J. Monahan a proposal was made, on 14 November 1912, that a paid secretary be appointed, with free bed and board and a salary of 100 guineas a year. The post was offered to Henry Harrison (1907).

This fundamental change not only initiated the process of placing the administration of the Club's affairs within a more professional framework but brought into prominence a relatively new member (Harrison had joined in 1907) whose impact upon and involvement with the SGC was to remain profound until his death in 1954. An outline of his achievements in public life would demand a chapter to itself; here it is pertinent to note that when he assumed the secretaryship he was well into his forties with a career as a Home Rule MP and active Parnellite behind him. Within two years, however, he was to opt for active military service and open an entirely new chapter in his life. With this move still before him he addressed himself, as Secretary, to overhauling the administrative structure, informing the Committee in July 1913 that, acting on the advice of Sir John P. Lynch, member and solicitor, he had arranged to have the Club land and buildings valued in the light of new Government regulations. In April he produced a scheme for reorganisation which was agreed to unanimously. When he was proposed for re-election by the Annual General Meeting on 1 February 1915 Lt. Col. Trevor Booth asked to be allowed to associate himself with the proposal and to express on behalf of himself and his brother Military Members, both permanent and temporary, his appreciation of the comfort and hospitality of the Club and the considerable improvement recently effected in its manage-

Maxwell Arnott *(Wills' 'Irish Sportsmen' cigarette card series, 1935):* 'Few trainers can claim to have saddled the winner of every important jumping event in Ireland . . . one of the leading lights of the All-Ireland polo club, while there is no more dashing member of the Ward and Meath Hunts'.

ment due to Harrison's attention. The report for 1914 recorded that the alterations and extensions involved were now complete (they included the new lavatory and cloakroom on the ground floor, the new smoking room lounge and alterations to the front hall) and noted a marked increase in the number of members lunching and dining. A table d'hote luncheon had been introduced at 1s 6d to supplement the à la carte.

The shadow of war nevertheless grew longer. In March 1915 it was resolved that Members on active service should pay their subscriptions as if they were on the Foreign List and that a Member answering for another at the Reading Out Dinner should be liable for the payment of his subscription only. A month later Henry Harrison advised the Committee that he had accepted a commission in the army and that since his future movements were likely to be uncertain, they should consider what steps they should take regarding his position and duties. The Committee, understandably, was reluctant to initiate any change; but this was forced upon them with Harrison's being ordered abroad in January 1916. He left with appreciation and good wishes to take up his duties with the Royal Irish Regiment in France. The Assistant Secretary was authorised to forward a cheque for £97 16s, the first instalment of a fund raised in the Club for the Regiment's Prisoner of War fund. In September Henry Harrison, wounded on active service and having in the short period of eight months been awarded the MC and bar, was on his way back to Ireland. The Committee agreed to recommend him to the next Annual General Meeting for Honorary Life Membership and in the meantime to offer him the same hospitality as was extended to other wounded officers staying in Dublin. He was to become almost immediately involved in Irish politics as a close associate of Horace Plunkett and to return to what he saw as his main life's work, the rehabilitation of the reputation of his beloved 'Chief', Charles Stewart Parnell.

The Derby Lottery and Dinner was not held in 1915. The report for the year recorded 'a certain shrinking in the expenditure of Members upon amusements', ascribing a worrying fall in revenue both to this factor and to generally increased costs. In June 1916 the Honorary Secretary (there had been as yet no permanent replacement for Henry Harrison) noted that takings for the first quarter of the year were seriously below those of the same period in 1915, and that 'to the end of April the reduction was £418, of which perhaps £100 were due to the Sinn Fein rising in Dublin. . .' Whether or not the employment of the description 'rising' rather than the more opprobrious 'rebellion' could be said to be noteworthy, this is the only reference to an event which, as far as Ireland was concerned, was to have repercussions greater even than those of the war, and to involve several prominent

Sir Lingard Goulding, Bart. (Will's 'Irish Sportsmen'). 'A leading member of the All-Ireland Polo Club, he gained International honours and was a member of the team which visited America in 1922 . . . one of the leading figures in the Irish financial world . . . also possessed considerable industrial interests in the country.

Club Members in major political roles. For the moment, however, the preoccupation was financial: in June 1916 the entrance fee for new members was suspended and the annual subscription for country members reduced, a move which caused John McCann, elected a Trustee the following year, to report the currency of rumours in Dublin detrimental to the Club regarding the apparent relaxation of entrance requirements. In September a 'war tax', not to exceed 2d in each shilling, was imposed on Members' bills and in the following January an Extraordinary General Meeting took a step seen by many as overdue and agreed to have future audits carried out by a chartered accountant. Thomas Geoghegan was appointed to this task in February.

If it might be considered supererogatory to refer to belt-tightening in the context of a social club the membership was obliged to acquiesce in certain measures resulting from economic conditions imposed by the war. It was agreed that packs of cards be played with a second time rather than discarded; and the Club led the way in a move in 1917 to curtail the consumption of food, its proposals for joint action in the matter having been declined by the Kildare Street, University and Friendly Brothers clubs. On a more serious note a special committee was formed in August to consider compiling a Roll of Honour based on a list prepared by Richard Martin (1890). Unfortunately no copy of this compilation would appear to have survived. The financial situation had improved by 1917, with the accounts back in surplus and membership again on the increase after a decline. The entrance fees were nevertheless still suspended in 1919 when, in July, W.J. White called attention to the very serious addition to the Club's expenses represented by the facts that income tax had risen to six shillings in the pound and that it had been the custom to pay interest on debentures free of tax. In this, the last year of hostilities as far as the world at large was concerned, the accounts were once more in the red. And Sir John Lynch discovered that under the terms of the lease the premises should be insured against storm and riot. . .

The 'Playboy' riots at the Abbey in 1907 were, in the event, to be no more than a shadow of things to come. In the meantime the Club membership was by no means entirely distanced from the generally peaceful revolution in the literary and artistic scene generally characterised as The Celtic Revival. One member, Laurence Waldron, MP, known to his wide circle of friends as 'Larkey', became in 1912 the first patron of the young stained-glass artist Harry Clarke, and remained so until his death in 1923: it was through him that the latter was introduced to many of his other customers and patrons. Waldron was by all accounts a larger-than-life figure in more senses than one: George Moore referred spitefully to his 'obscene bulk', but Gogarty painted a kindlier picture of the man: 'I admit that Larkey is a sub-

William Butler Yeats

stantial man; he weighs four hundred pounds and over, but then he is a stockbroker to the Catholic church. . . Larkey has to do sums for the bishops and archbishops and invest money for the Little Sisters of the Poor. He lives sumptuously in a beautiful house on Killiney Hill. Yes, Larkey is a great fellow in every sense. He sits in his office in Anglesea Street with two telephones and four mantelpieces by Bossi in the room. . . He wears a skullcap of black silk topped by a large pink rhododendron. He hasn't seen his feet for years'.

Gogarty was not an SGC member himself – unlike his son Oliver D., SC – but the membership at the time included the novelist Stephen Gwynn and, until his translation to Kildare Street ('I wonder what possessed that wise man to become a member of such an establishment' – Gogarty again), the poet W.B. Yeats. Elected a Member of the SGC in 1914, Yeats was, as the Great War drew to a close, moving into one of his most productive periods – and engaged in moving himself and his new wife to the tower in Ballylee which was to figure so significantly in his later poems. In 1918 he was planning a series of lectures in the Abbey Theatre. On 11 April he wrote from Coole Park, the home of Lady Gregory, to his Dublin agent, Mrs James Duncan: 'You have no doubt made some arrangements with [the Abbey Secretary] about the necessary attendance for Sunday, or for someone-else to do so. I shall reach Dublin Saturday evening and stay at the Stephen's Green Club. Sorry to give you so much trouble'.

He arrived in Dublin to find the city in the grip of an influenza epidemic, to which he himself became a victim. He wrote to Mrs Duncan:

Sunday/Stephen's Green Club/Dublin

Dear Mrs Duncan: I have had 24 hours of fever and cold. I am better but am too weak to go to lecture tonight. So committee and its sec. must take charge.

As ever/W.B. Yeats

It cannot be said, however, that Yeats apart, the Club membership was markedly associated with the arts. Most of the names speak of politics rather than poetry, litigation rather than literature, with a strong representation from among the long-established Dublin mercantile and professional families – Arnott, Cochrane, Goodbody, Harrington, Martin, Pim, Power, and others. Medical men, bankers and stockbrokers are also well represented, with names in each of these professional categories which resonated in spheres beyond the Club confines as they became associated with the major public issues of the day. The ivory gavel of the Irish Convention of 1917 – one of the many failed attempts to find an Irish solution to an Irish problem – was one of Horace Plunkett's most treasured possessions, and one of the few remaining to him after his house, Kilteragh, Foxrock, was burned during the Civil War. When he resigned from the Senate of the Irish Free State, to which he had been appointed in 1922, a fellow Club member and Senator, Sir Thomas Grattan Esmonde, said of him: 'I think it is a great pity when our country is struggling to her feet that the Senate should lose the services of a man who had given his whole life with absolute disinterestedness to further Irish interests'.

Grattan Esmonde himself came of a Co. Wexford family long associated with the Club, and there are several other instances of succeeding generations of membership. James Owen Wylie, Member 1885, was a distinguished judge who played a dominant role in Club affairs; his nephew, W.E. Wylie, (1908) was to find himself, after the 1916 rising, acting as prosecuting counsel at the courts martial of the captured leaders. There is something of a mystery, as the late Leon O Broin points out in his book *W.E. Wylie and the Irish Revolution,* concerning the prosecution of de Valera, in which Wylie was apparently not involved. In a letter on Club notepaper written in 1964 – the year of his death – Wylie said 'I think I should record an incident that happened yesterday. In the anteroom before the Punchestown lunch the President [de Valera] spoke to me and said: "You prosecuted in 1916, and a man is enquiring from me at present what I said and how I defended myself at the time. I cannot recollect anything about it, or who was there or what was said"'. Wylie replied that he was not prosecuted at the time and there were nothing to remember and there the conversation ended.

Wylie retired from the General Committee on 16 February 1920 and was appointed a High Court Judge in November under a warrant from King George V; (he was again offered a judgeship in June 1924, this time by the Governor-General of the Irish Free State). On 3 October 1922 he was appointed, with Sir George Fotterell and John McCann, to a sub-committee to 'consider the affairs of the Club with special reference to the question of economical and efficient working of the club and the necessity for the appointment of a paid whole-time secretary or manager or both'. Following the death of his wife during the Second World War he sold his residence, Clonsilla House, and took up permanent residence in the Stephen's Green Club.

Postwar conditions had already imposed change on the conduct of the Club and its internal arrangements. An initiative to increase the wages of the staff met with a grateful response, a letter to the Secretary, G.V. Martyn, on 8 March 1919 stating that 'we fully realise what this extra expense means to the Club and we assure you that our best efforts will be faithfully discharged in carrying out our duties'. The accounts for the year were in profit, largely due to the retention of the 'War Measures' which included the War Tax already referred to and higher charges for wine, spirits and minerals. The entrance fee was reimposed as from June of that year and in November 1920, in the wake of a thorough financial examination by the House Committee, the subscription was increased. The War Tax was discontinued as from 1 January 1921. Social changes, too, were in the air: smoking of pipes was permitted in the Coffee Room after dinner and in July 1921 it was agreed that ladies should be admitted as luncheon and dinner guests on special occasions – a hesitant step down a road not as yet fully traversed.

In October 1922 it was proposed that a paid secretary-manager, a Member of the Club, be appointed and accorded board, salary and room, as recommended by the sub-committee under W.E. Wylie. His salary was to be £100 per annum, but the recommendation was not accepted by the Extraordinary General Meeting of 13 November, which did, however, agree on the appointment of a House Steward, and this position was advertised in the Dublin daily papers and the London *Times* and *Daily Telegraph*. As the year closed the Committee was considering the applications of six candidates from among a very large number of respondents. The report for 1922 alluded to a considerable reduction in the number of dinners served during the second half of the year, 'owing to the disturbed condition of the city'.

W.E. Wylie's close friend James MacMahon (1919), Under-Secretary to the Lord Lieutenant and subsequently a Privy Counsellor, was to play a major role in the setting up of the Free State that was to emerge from the chaos of war. Wylie wrote of him: 'His sanity and calm, his complete sincerity and his understanding of Irish problems has helped me time out of number', whilst Andy Cope, who himself played a major role in Anglo-Irish negotiations, wrote to MacMahon: 'I must tell you that if there is any credit due to anyone for setting up the Free State, it is due to you and you alone. . .'. The birth of the Free State, however, was far from painless. On 23 February 1920 a curfew was imposed in requiring 'persons within the Dublin Metropolitan Police District to remain indoors between the hours of 12 o'clock midnight and 5 o'clock a.m.' Thought the restriction was slightly eased in June and again in November, the report for 1920 noted that 'the disturbed state of the country, and in particular the advance of the curfew to 10 p.m. from 23rd November 1920 have had a prejudicial effect on the use of the Club by Members. . .' In October of that year the appropriate authorities were requested to remove some firearms apparently left on the premises by Members. During the first half of the following year, with the curfew still in force, the drop in the numbers using the Club gave rise to apprehension but following the Truce in the Anglo-Irish war which came into effect on 11 July the recovery, according to the report for the year, was 'rapid'.

Ireland – and Dublin – had, however, much still to endure as the Civil War which followed the cessation of Anglo-Irish hostilities wreaked further devastation both in material and human terms. Internecine strife replaced the broader confrontation, and in February 1922 the Committee decided that no toasts of any kind should be proposed at Club dinners until further notice. In May it was agreed that in view of the disturbed conditions the contemplated closing for renovation and redecoration should be postponed. A letter from the secretary of the Kildare Street Club requested that their members be invited to use the Stephen's Green Club whilst their own house was forcibly occupied; but it was pointed out that under Rule 9 an Extraordinary General Meeting would be necessary before such a request could be acceded to.

The matter came before a Special General Meeting on 29 May 1922, W. Barrington Jellett in the chair. Sir George Fotterell told the meeting that the University Club had already issued an invitation to Kildare Street members and the use of a room as an office for their secretary. He then outlined possible objections to Stephen's Green adopting a similar course: that the issuing of an invitation might involve the Club in the seizure of its own premises; that such an invitation might meet with a rebuff; and that the premises did not afford the requisite accommodation. He was nevertheless of the opinion that an invitation should be issued and that 'such action would best uphold the Dignity and Welfare of the Stephen's Green Club'.

The discussion which followed was revealing both of the civic tensions then prevailing and of the perceived character of the two clubs. Thomas L. Plunkett urged members to support the move and in so doing to 'remove the possibility of outsiders considering that a refusal to extend hospitality was for religious reasons'. Lord Justice O'Connor, opposing, regretted the introduction of the religious issue and expressed himself of the opinion that 'the Members of the Kildare Street Club considered themselves of a class above the class of the Members of the Stephen's Green Club', suggesting that they had never offered to extend the courtesy of hospitality. R.A. Anderson said that it was in no way a matter of religion, simply a 'friendly act', a view supported by Mr Justice Wylie, who believed that all prejudices should be sunk and that it would be 'the sporting thing to do'. This attitude prevailed, and the resolution was carried with two dissentients.

'The blinds is down, Joxer': on 15 December 1922 the Committee learnt of the impending final closure of the Sackville Street Club which had been in existence since the 1790s and resolved that any of its members wishing to become candidates for membership of the SGC should not be required to pay an entrance fee should they be elected before 1 March 1923. It is not on record that the offer to a membership of stolid Unionist persuasion was widely availed of. Though tinged perhaps with self-interest, the move could, nevertheless, fairly be described as 'the sporting thing to do'. The gesture, occurring as it did a week after the coming into existence of the Irish Free State, was suggestive both of courage and continuity in the face of drastic social and political changes – changes which were to find the Club not, perhaps, altogether certain of the role it was to play in the new Ireland.

In the Saddle

PHILIP O'CONNOR

Appearances can be deceptive. The quiet atmosphere of the Stephen's Green Club seems an unlikely gathering place for horsemen. The reality is that for generations Members have been associated with horses, horse racing, and, in particular, hunting. This short contribution to the Club's history will touch on some aspects of Members' involvement with horses including the remarkable connection with the Ward Union Stag Hounds.

Philip O'Connor

In the year of the Club's sesquicentennial celebrations it is difficult for us to adjust our thoughts to the conditions prevailing in Ireland at and after the time of the Famine. The lack of opportunity, indeed the wholesale deprivation suffered by so many in rural Ireland must dictate an overall sense of great sadness when one considers and reflects on those times. For certain elements of society shortages were unknown and prosperity continued unabated. This was so for many in the eastern part of the country and certainly was so for those actively involved in professional and business life. That prosperity spawned the origins of the Club and also many other cultural and recreational organisations about the middle of the 19th century in Ireland.

For a city club with a largely city or suburban membership it is interesting to note direct links between Stephen's Green Club and such groups as the All Ireland Polo Club, clubs associated with Leopardstown, Punchestown and Fairyhouse Racecourses and various packs of hounds in or about Dublin and the adjoining counties. Many readers will enquire as to the relevance of the Ward Union Hunt in reference to the activities of Club members. The Hunt originated about 1830 and following an amalgamation with the Dublin Garrison Hounds about 1854 produced the present Ward Union Stag Hounds hunting North County Dublin and Meath, with which pack there has been singular and continuing involvement by Club Members over generations.

83

Fred Clarke, Clerk of Leopardstown Racecourse (1) with William Beckett, father of Samuel *(Eoin O'Brien: 'The Beckett Country')*.

One early marker that will be of interest is the first running of the Ward Union Hunt Cup in 1867 over a prepared course at the present Fairyhouse venue in County Meath. This race replaced a straight point-to-point which had been held for many years across country and which had been known from the early days of the Hunt as the Teapot Race, presumably by reason of the trophy awarded to the winner.

Another identifying link in our early equestrian records is the engraving presently in the hallway of the Club, which is a copy of the William Osborne painting of the Field at a Ward Union Meet in 1873. It is unusual in that it incorporates identification of approximately 35 members in accordance with the key which hangs immediately below the engraving. The copy in the Club was presented to it by T. Levins Moore in 1927. Why was such a painting commissioned? Where was the meet? Was it perhaps at one of the delightfully named venues of today such as 'The Snailbox' or 'The Dancing Tree'? Perhaps in the family records of some Club Member there are records that would fascinate the historian and the sportsman.

A precise record of Members from the early days is not available from Club sources. Other material however gives us the information that T. Levins Moore was a Club Member at the turn of the century. He went on to become Master of the Ward Union for six years, immediately after World War I. Interestingly, his son was none other

84

than Andrew Moore (1932) who was similarly a Ward Union Master of Hounds between 1939 and 1947. Between father and son another distinguished Club Member filled the role of Master of the same pack for 14 Seasons, namely Judge William Wylie. The Judge (1908), needs no introduction in this note. He gave generously of his time and effort in supporting the objectives of the Royal Dublin Society over very many years with particular emphasis on the encouragement of the half-bred horse, through the medium of International Show Jumping at Ballsbridge. The Judge was also Chairman of the Racing Board in 1945/1946. In recent years four other Members of the Club have held the position of Master or Joint Master of the Wards, namely G.V. Malcomson, Standish Collen, Denis Coakley and more recently Raymond Keogh.

Other avenues of enquiry disclose a solid connection between the Club and the All Ireland Polo Club. For example, T. Levins Moore was its Honorary Secretary at the turn of the century. The Leonard Family of Culmullen, County Meath, themselves comprised an All Ireland Polo Club Team in the 1920s. That team included Jack (1928) and his father John Leonard, who also managed to fit in a great deal of work at Ballsbridge in his capacity as Honorary Secretary of the Royal Dublin Society over many years. He was a member also of the Sackville Club until it closed its doors in 1922. On its demise it transferred the luncheon facilities at Punchestown Racecourse to our then Trustees Thomas L. Plunkett, Matthew Barrington Jellett and John McCann.

Many in the accountancy profession will learn with interest that Robert (later Sir Robert) Gardner, who was born in 1838, was not only a founding Partner of the accountancy firm of Craig Gardner, but is also recorded as being a Member of both the Club and the Ward Union Hunt in the early years of the century. At that time he was living at Ashley, Clyde Road, and with his contemporaries quite probably hacked his hunter from there to meets at such places as Finglas, then very much in the country. The writer can readily remember attending meets of the South County Dublin Harriers at Rathfarnham and Chapelizod in the early 1950s. At that time it was quite commonplace for hunters to be hacked, for example, from Kellett's yard at Mespil Road to meets in County Dublin. In the early part of the century travel to meets at greater distances from Dublin was often by way of special hunting trains that transported both horse and rider. The departure times of these were arranged specifically to suit the day's hunting arrangements. No information is available as to the railway timetable for the return journey: presumably, the guard on the train had a certain discretion.

Post World War II the riding tradition in the Club continued with

Tony Brindley

men like Seamus Woods and Norman Chance, the latter driving an open sports car to Hunt meets in mid-winter. The distinguished obstetrician Dr Bethel Solomons was another active member of both the Club and the Ward Union. Those hunting about that time will no doubt recall his attire on a wet day when he sported not only the customary black tall hat and black hunting coat, but also a huge waterproof knee apron secured by small straps at the back of each knee; it was an immensely practical arrangement, but one that is seldom now seen. He really loved his hunting and regaled many a gathering with amusing anecdotes from the hunting field. He liked to recall the American hunting visitor who on his first day in Meath eagerly set about finding out the names of the key hunt personnel. His eyes soon lit on the craggy yet distinguished face of Bethel and immediately he enquired as to the identity of this rider. On being informed that this was Solomons, the Master of the Rotunda, he replied with gusto that he must arrange a day with the Rotunda Hounds!

Another amusing tale allegedly attributed to the doctor is the story concerning the busy suburban curate, Father Jimmy, who was hearing confessions on a Saturday evening. Long before the word 'ecumenism' was in vogue the same spirit was afoot in the hunting field. The good curate was able to facilitate a lady follower of another persuasion by granting to her the facility of parking her bicycle in the church porch while she took the number 10 bus from the terminus across the city to the famous livery yard of Bill Magee at Montpellier Hill at the other number 10 terminus. In these times shortage of petrol and lack of horse boxes often gave rise to lengthy return journeys from a day's hunting. The story goes that Father Jimmy, himself a well known Ward follower, was busily engaged in his confessional. He pricked his ears at the sound of a released bicycle lock and chain when they rattled tellingly on the spokes of the bicycle wheel. The startled penitent, his contrition augmented by Father Jimmy's questioning, was amazed beyond belief when the next question emerged in a loud stage whisper, "Did you catch the Deer . . .?" Neither the penitent's response nor his penance are recorded.

Animal lovers will be glad to know that the deer will normally run to a river or stream and is then captured and returned to the safety of the deer park.

Another interesting link between the two clubs arises via the Brindley family. Basil, the Chairman of our Sesquicentennial Committee is an avid Ward follower, like his stockbroker father Tony (1932). The Brindley connection with the Ward Union can be traced back for five

A Club Christmas card showing Charles Brindley (1817-1879) riding to hounds, based on the painting by Michael Angelo Hayes in the National Gallery.

generations to Charles, who was Turf Club Keeper of the Match Book and in turn through Jim, who carried the horn for some 30 seasons back to Charles Brindley, who acted as Huntsman for over 20 years until a short time prior to his death in 1879. An obelisk erected by popular subscription following his death stands to this day a short distance north of the Ashbourne-Dublin Road, close to the ninth milestone. The rotund figure of Charles was the subject of a chalk drawing (now in the National Gallery) by Michael Angelo Hayes who is remembered for his engravings of the Bianconi horse-drawn coaches.

We must be indebted to the author of a small booklet giving a concise history of the Ward Union Hounds and published many years ago. In congratulating Jim Brindley on the control of his hounds he writes: 'to judge of the control Jim has over his hounds one should go and see them feeding. The whole pack are brought into the feeding yard, then the day's repast is wheeled in, in feeding troughs; the hungry hounds run round, sniff and lick the edges, but not a hound attempts to feed until Jim says Grace. He may delay five or ten minutes but it is only when he says "for what we are about to receive. . . . ." that you see nothing but sterns'. Thankfully such control is not required at the Members' table in the Club today!

Overall one gets the impression that the proximity of the Wards to the City of Dublin, the challenging nature of the terrain, and above all the cut and thrust of finding one's way across big natural fences appears to have procured the attention and loyalty of Members of the Club in successive generations; it remains so to this day.

A hunting yarn was told frequently and with considerable glee by Gerry Burke Kennedy (1965), who was a manager with the old Hibernian Bank. One day there was a most urgent telephone enquiry from Head Office to his rural branch. The bank porter felt it prudent to maintain a certain confidentiality in reference to the manager's absence in the hunting field. In reply to a searching question from the Area Inspector the porter merely indicated that his boss was at a funeral. When pressed for details including the name of the deceased the porter replied "one of the Foxes of Streamstown Sir. . .".

Interestingly, in a city club, there are still many who are currently hunting including two Masters of Foxhounds, namely Martin Clancy the Master of the Shillelagh; and George Younghusband, the Master of the Ormond and amongst the more senior Club Members there are quite a number who have been active huntsmen including John Dunne, Paddy and Dick Duggan, Vincent and Eugene Davy, Tom Wall, Ken O'Reilly Hyland, John Carrigan, John Corcoran and An Taoiseach, C. J. Haughey. All of this is probably not so surprising when one considers that there is such an active tradition within the Club relating

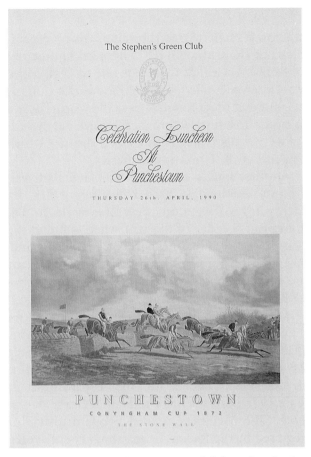

The Stephen's Green Club

Celebration Luncheon At Punchestown

THURSDAY 26th. APRIL. 1990

PUNCHESTOWN

CONYNGHAM CUP 1872

THE STONE WALL

Sesquicentennial luncheon menu cover for the Punchestown Meeting

to horses and when one considers that the major social function in the Club year remains the Grand National Dinner.

On the thoroughbred side there have been many and varied links with all aspects of racing. Club Members bred many significant animals and were and are widely involved in the industry and in the administration of the sport, including service with such bodies as the Royal Dublin Society, the Racing Board and the Turf Club. Lord Killanin, a member since 1950, followed his service as President of the International Olympic Committee from 1972 to 1980 by acting as chairman of a commission of inquiry into the thoroughbred horse breeding industry at the request of the Government. The report, published in July 1986, contained a wealth of detail together with far sighted recommendations for the future.

Philip Love of Marlay Grange, Rathfarnham (1950) was the breeder of Larkspur, the Epsom Derby Winner in 1962. He was also the leading Irish vendor and breeder for many years at Goff's Bloodstock Sales which took place on the site of the present banking headquarters in Ballsbridge. Some readers may find it hard to credit that I can recall attending also at a Goff's Sales premises in Lower Mount Street adjoining Holles Street Hospital. An observant eye can even today pick out the name 'Goff's' engraved in dust on its facade. Mention of Robert J. Goff & Co. leads one to Cyril Myerscough (1944) who was closely identified with the Bloodstock Company and was a steward at a number of racecourses over the years. Those attending Irish Management Institute lectures at Clonard, Sandyford will be interested to know that his father Fred trained the 1943 Irish Derby winner The Phoenix at the family home there.

Another highly successful Club member was Dick Ball of Naul, County Dublin. He bred Ballymoss, which, having won the Irish Derby in 1957 went on a year later to elevate Dick to the position of European breeder of the year when winning the Eclipse Stakes, the King George and Queen Elizabeth Stakes and finally the Prix de L'Arc de Triomphe. It is no coincidence that Larkspur and Ballymoss are both examples of the successes of the legendary trainer Vincent O'Brien who was a member of the Club for a number of years.

Leopardstown Racecourse is strongly supported by Club Members. This perpetuates a trend which commenced in 1888 when on the inauguration of the Leopardstown Club, Stephen's Green Club Members were automatically accepted without ballot. National Hunt devotees will be familiar with the Leopardstown Handicap Chase which since 1977 bears the name of Harold Clarke. He and later his son, Fred, both Club Members, guided Leopardstown from 1912 until it was acquired by the Racing Board about twenty years ago.

No attempt has been made in this note to describe particular hunting experiences or to attempt to record individual winning or indeed losing runners or owners. There will however be one recent exception which serves well to illustrate the bond between the Club and the horse. At Leopardstown the 1985 Winner of 'the Harold Clarke Handicap Chase' was Seskin Bridge, the property of the Irish National Stud, running in the colours of that most distinguished Club Member, His Excellency The President of Ireland, Doctor Patrick Hillery.

Hopefully this contribution, which seeks to string together some areas of inter-connection between the Stephen's Green Club and the horse will hold the attention of those with only a passing interest. Equally it is hoped that it will rekindle for others a glowing memory of some valued equine friend. There are many Club members who have had over decades the exhilarating challenge of riding to hounds. That remains one of the great sporting experiences. I conclude this note having had today such an experience: a day with the Ward Union, a point of some seven miles, fourteen as hounds ran.

23rd day of February 1990

Wooden Walls

NIALL P. HIGGINS

Squash in the Stephen's Green Club goes back to 1910 when the court was built. Unfortunately there remain very few records of the 80 years of young athletes, ageing and middle-aged enthusiasts, and pre-geriatric sportsmen who chased around its hallowed walls.

The Squash Court was preceded by a Racquets Court. The Club Minutes of 1875 make reference to damage to 'McKenzie's premises' by racquet balls. In 1888 they refer to the Racquets Court being derelict for 20 years, which would seem to be a contradiction of the earlier entry. The Racquets Court appears to have been what is now the southern bay of the Royal Irish Automobile Club garage and may have been jointly used with the Hibernian United Services Club.

The Stephen's Green Club Squash Court is unusual in that it has three flexible wooden walls and only the front wall of solid plaster. Add to this the fact that it is under-sized by to-day's standards and you have a situation which gave the home team an advantage but wasn't too helpful when playing away.

Niall P. Higgins

Support for squash in the Club has always followed a cyclical pattern – for a while a number of youngish members would create an active and competitive group: as they grew older interest would slacken until new blood got things moving again.

Up to 30 years ago there was only a limited number of squash courts in the country. For many years the Club fielded a team in the league and won it in c. 1957. There were many enjoyable matches against Trinity, Bankers, University Club, Friendly Brothers, Aer Lingus, The Curragh, and especially Guinness, where the Court was located behind the 'Brewer's House' in James's Street. Any dehydration suffered during the game was more than replenished afterwards by unlimited supplies of the Black Stuff! In the 1960s the Club also fielded an A Team, which was composed of members who in their earlier days had played for Fitzwilliam. This period was probably the most active time of the Club's squash in the last half century. There is a very fine trophy for the Club Squash Championship, and a list of winners is appended. It is not inclusive of all the best players in the Club as the competition was a social event and often heavily weighted in favour of the outsider, as the writer can confirm. On one occasion the committee organising the Championship 'phoned around for entrants and only discovered at the Dinner that one of the finalists was not a member of the Club at all and had been invited by mistake, an error which did nothing to lessen the enjoyment of all those present.

Maintaining an old squash court is an ongoing problem and the calls on the Committee for funds were not always met with universal enthusiasm. On one occasion a senior member enquired would the squash players provide their labour if the Club provided the material. When the squash representative responded as to whether the same system would apply to repairs to the Card Room, the necessary funds were provided without further opposition.

Perhaps for many the most enduring memory of Stephen's Green squash is the shower in the changing rooms! Still in position to-day it is a masterpiece of Victorian plumbing which can rightly claim preservation status with the Georgian ceilings of the Club. It was a forerunner of to-day's hydrotherapy: apart from bombarding the torso from all angles it could also be used, by careful use of the control, as a weapon to hit the next user with an icy blast, or by leaving the door of the shower open, to shoot out into the changing room and drench any clothes left in its path.

The fact that the trophy has not been played for since 1981 may be a reflection of the cyclical interest in the game but also of the increase in recent years in the number of other courts available in the city and also of their quality. Perhaps the advent of the Club's 150th Anniversary will be the occasion of a renewal of activity in the Squash Court.

STEPHEN'S GREEN SQUASH RACQUETS CUP.
Presented by J.O. McCall

1912	Capt. D.W. Kelly.
1913	J. McCann.
1914	J. McCann.
1923	F.J. Lillis.
1934	David O'Meara.
1935	David O'Meara.
1953	T.P. Hogan.

1959	T. Wall.
1960	D. Pigot.
1962	R. O'Reilly.
1963	H.W. Hamilton.
1964	J.D. Hackett.
1966	W. Galen Weston.
1975	D. Pigot, K. McGilligan, J. McDonagh.
1977	I. Cairnduff.
1978	Niall P. Higgins.
1979	P. O'B Butler.
1980	P. O'B Butler.
1981	David Ennis.

Amongst Club Members who served as officers of the Irish Squash Racquets Association are the following: Presidents – 1935/37, The Hon. Mr. Justice Cahir Davitt; 1944/45. A.L. Moore 1946/47, T.A. Brindley; 1957/8, W.A. Sandys; 1961/2 S. Monahan; Honorary Secretaries: 1938/39, W.A. Sandys; 1949/50, E.W. McCabe; 1951/4, S. Monahan; 1956/59, B. Kilcoyne.

Plus ça change . . . : 1922–1945

NIALL O'KELLY

Niall O'Kelly

The years from 1922 to 1945 may be thought of loosely as an inter-war period, some four years after the end of the First World War, followed by 'the Troubles' in this country and spanning recessionary times to the end of World War II. With the exception of the lighter times in the '30s these were quite difficult years and included notable political changes in this country and, of course, the appearance of our new Constitution. There were also periods of unrest with strikes afoot, and Britain, to whom our currency was then tied, going off the Gold Standard. The dollar was four to the pound.

In a review by Ronan Keane of Brendan Sexton's *Ireland and the Crown 1922–1936. The Governor-Generalship of the Irish Free State* a number of interesting references are made:

> Hard to believe that during the lifetime of many of us, there was a Governor-General in the Phoenix Park, the representative of the King-Emperor, giving the royal assent to Bills enacted in Leinster House. At the very time in the early 1930s when the British Empire had extended its frontiers to what were to prove its utmost limits, its first and most wayward colony was busy dismantling the whole imperial apparatus.

> At the time of the treaty the issues which provoked the deepest differences between the Irish and British sides – and later the Treaty among the Irish themselves – were membership of the British Empire, and the oath of allegiance. Compared with these topics, which touched raw nerves on both sides, questions as to the precise status of the King's representative might seem of small account.

> Mr. Sexton's scholarly and lucid account of the evolution and ultimate disappearance of the office of Governor-General show how far from the case this was at the time. The insistence of the British side that the office should be the constitutional apex of the Irish Free State and the physical embodiment of the imperial crown was met

with dogged attempts on the Irish side to whittle it away to a nullity.

The prospects of a continuation of the same regime in an independent state was repellent. Nor were matters helped by the suspicion on the Irish side that the British would insist on the office being held, as had been the case with the Viceroy, by an English peer or, worse still, a member of the royal family. In the Dail debates on the Treaty, one deputy who opposed it claimed that there was a plot on foot to arrange a marriage between Princess Mary, a daughter of George the Fifth, and Michael Collins, and to install Collins as the first Governor-General.

The eventual appointment of the third and last Governor-General, Domhnall ua Buachalla, 'who owned a shop in Maynooth' was not calculated to placate the British. Their anxieties can hardly have been relieved by the valiant diplomacy of the High Commissioner in London, John Dulanty, who described him as the owner of 'an emporium in the ecclesiastical capital of Ireland.'

It is in the context of such a background that the Club in this period must be viewed. There are many present Members who will recall these stirring times; they may not necessarily have been Members at the time, in fact few enough will have been. Naturally the Club minutes do not go into these happenings: the Club took them in its stride. The two war periods bracketing this period experienced severe rationing of all commodities which, as far as a Club is concerned, mostly involved food and fuel. Transport restrictions were also severe

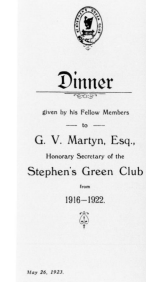

Dinner

given by his Fellow Members
— to —
G. V. Martyn, Esq.,
Honorary Secretary of the
Stephen's Green Club
from
1916–1922.

May 26, 1923.

VINS

Old Solera, 1870

Champagne

Pol. Roger.   Vintage 1914.
In Magnums.

Port

Cockburns   1896
Taylors   1900

Liqueurs

Brandy—Hine, 1863.
Grand Marnier,
Chartreuse, Benedictine, &c.

Cigars.   Cigarettes.

MENU

Hors d'Œuvres varies

Consommé Printanier
Crème de Volaille

Saumon Froid. Mayonnaise
Salade de Concombres

Noisette d'Agneau
Haricots Verts   Pommes Nouvelles

Jambon de York au Champagne
Epinards

Cailles Rotie
Salade

Asperges au Beurre.

Vanilla Pouding glacé à la Cognac
Fruits gelée's Maraschino

Œufs à la Russe

Dessert.

Café.

Menu of the dinner given to G.V. Martyn, Honorary Secretary, 1916-22, by his fellow Members, 26 May 1923.

William Evelyn Wylie

on accessibility of the Club to its Members giving rise to greater bedroom occupancy.

As might be expected the Membership list contained a high number of service personnel returned from the war, many with decorations after distinguished service overseas. There were captains and colonels; including a Colonel O'Sullivan of the Connaught Rangers, the father of Maureen O'Sullivan, the famous film actress.

In the early '20s the Membership list showed many being transferred to the Foreign list due to overseas postings in the services. Of course there were many returning to what was to become a very different world, and much Committee time seems to have been taken up with all these transfers as well as fixing the appropriate levels of subscription rates for variously broken periods.

All of these toings and froings seem to have been overcome satisfactorily and the Club settled into what might be called a consolidation period with all of the normal activities proceeding apace. Apart from the main facilities provided and much availed of, being lunch and dinner, and of course accommodation, there were very many supporters of the bridge table, billiards, and squash rackets. These activities are still popularly followed with tournaments every year. Billiards, however universal previously, has now been replaced entirely by snooker, perhaps then not thought to be such a gentleman's game.

It is worth noting that the Squash Court was erected in 1910 at a cost of £216.3.0 by Members' subscriptions. It has survived well considering that it is of construction that would scarcely be considered today. Eventually the roof developed some leaks, causing a rather slippery floor. Some thirty years ago the Squash players pointed this out to the Committee requesting that immediate repairs be put in hand. The Committee in its constant endeavour to avoid or limit expenditure suggested that as the Squash players were an active group they should carry out the necessary work themselves with the Club providing the materials. Needless to say this would be a hard decision to bring back to the players and did not bode well for the continuation of the game. Undaunted, the players' delegate pointed out to the Committee that there was also a leak in the Card Room roof and it was presumed that the same onus would not fall on the bridge players most of whom were venerable and not really in what might be called the active category. This argument naturally carried the day and the repairs were duly effected.

One should not pass by the references to squash without referring to the changing room in which about that time a magnificient shower room was erected. The shower bath has to be experienced to be believed, as Niall P. Higgins recalls on p. 92. It is noted that occasionally members having to change in town before going to an outside dinner utilise this facility often, no doubt wishing that it could be availed of after rather than before.

Arthur Cox

The available minutes make it clear that the Committee throughout this time was not really autocratic but it was firm – especially on any serious matters. It was also rigid on the limitations of its own powers and on several occasions ruled that action it was called on to take would be ultra vires. It felt itself as bound by the Club Rules as it called on the Members to be.

The General Committee consisted of sixteen Members; five further constituted a House Committee. This apparently worked well, although more than once a conflict arose as to just how independent of the Committee the House Committee was. This is supposed to imply that broader matters of principle were being shouldered by the House Committee thus leaving, on these issues, the main body of the Committee potentially bypassed. Naturally the Committee established the true position, that the House Committee was a sub-committee, and indeed the House Committee at times referred matters to the General Committee for further clarification, as the following extract from the minutes will illustrate.

In 1923, with Judge Wylie moved to the Chair, the minutes' record was as follows:-

The Chairman intimated that the House Committee had received from Mr. Duncan his resignation of his post as Assistant Secretary.

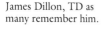

James Dillon, TD as many remember him.

Arising from it the Chairman read to the meeting the Recommendations made by the House Committee . . . which as regards Mr. Duncan were that his resignation be accepted, and that he be granted one year's salary as recognition of his long and faithful service. Mr. Campbell asked if it were in the power of the House or of the General Committee, to make such a payment.

The Chairman read the Rule as to the powers of the House Committee and stated that it appeared that the House Committee had the power, but it nevertheless decided to refer the matter to the General Committee.

A discussion followed and Sir George Fottrell stated that it had been the custom for matters of policy to be dealt with by the General Committee and matters of administration etc. by the House Committee.

The Chairman next read the recommendation of the House Committee as to the combining of the duties hitherto carried out by Mr. Duncan and the duties hitherto carried out by Miss Withers in the person of a Clerk – sex unspecified.

The closing wording of this extract may require a second reading to arrive at the true meaning and intent. Over 100 replies were received to an advertisement to fill this vacancy.

This Committee meeting appears to have been a busy one for it also decided to delegate to the Derby Sweep Sub-Committee to decide 'from the number dining at the Derby Dinner, what amount of wine is to be charged to the Sweep Fund'. At this meeting also it was decided that an offer of £150 (which included £30 worth of china etc.) should be made to the Sackville Street Club for the Punchestown Luncheon Hut. This was in response to information received as to availability.

About this time a row erupted between the General Committee and the House Committee on the question of decoration of the Club premises. A sum of £1,000 was the House Committee target, but in response to their circular only £233.19.0 was subscribed. The publication of this list was delayed 'pending the receipt of subscriptions from the Trustees and other prominent Members of the Club.' A Committee circular followed which the House Committee felt was 'a slight on their probity and capacity and renders entirely nugatory their appointment of a Decoration Committee.' They also complained that it was proposed 'to appoint custodians of the fund and to advise on its employment.' There were claimed as a result to be two Decoration Funds and two bodies to administer them – *plus ça change, plus c'est la même chose*! The House Committee requested the General Committee to call a 'Special General Meeting at which their resignation may be accepted.'

A Committee meeting in 1924 received a Report of Committee of Enquiry into a loss of £1,318 and held twelve sittings. Notable was the item of Sundry House Repairs which had risen from £88 in 1922 to £413 in 1923. 'On looking over Messrs. Fletcher & Philipson's Account we observe that their men appear to have been working in the Club almost every day during the year. We think that much closer supervision . . .' Coffee Room returns under enquiry showed that although receipts from sales were down by £276, the amount expended on the purchase of provisions was up by £276, 'and this notwithstanding that food prices were generally lower in 1923 than in 1922.'

This report was wide ranging and called for a change in management, and for quarterly reports to the Trustees and General Committee. It went on to enquire about the by now famous Decorations Fund reporting that no replies could be obtained from the Hon. Secretary over a period of months in spite of frequent written requests and 'since then we have heard nothing from him.' They wanted to know about liabilities incurred and doubtless this matter resolved itself. This was evidently a difficult period and a further meeting shortly afterwards had troubles about the cost of food purchases and price setting with the House Steward stating that

Gordon Bennett ('Spy' cartoon from 'Vanity Fair').

he did not know the cost of the meals he had been supplying against the prices in the Dining Room and that he could not get the prices of some articles bought in. Matters appear to have been taken in hand and the catering accounts improved. These events led up to Debenture issue, which question was to occupy much Committee time over a long period following.

We cannot pass from reference to Committee activities without mentioning Judge Wylie, who had served on the General Committee from before this period right up to the mid '60s. While he was one of many very distinguished Committee men he was one who will be remembered most of the 'old brigade' and the best known to many present Members. Though he may have appeared to some as particularly rigid he was a very fair and approachable man and a great raconteur. He possessed grip where grip was called for.

Frederick Boland in his capacity as Chancellor of Dublin University.

An unofficial title appeared in the records in these halcyon days and that was 'Father of the House'. It was adopted in at least two instances and was obviously bestowed only on rare occasions. The title appears to have been used for the venerable and long-lived who had served a very long time on the Committee. In the case of one of these gentlemen he was over 60 years a Member.

There was almost complete immobility of the people on the Committee and there was no rotational resignation arrangement. Any reasonable attendance virtually ensured re-election and the composition of the Committee remained with little change over many years, despite an annual election.

There was much evidence of General Meetings and adjourned General Meetings and at these a very full turn-out was usual with wide ranging discussions of the matters in hand. Based on available records most of the decisions emerging from these meetings were balanced and appropriate. On some occasions these meetings were adjourned to a reconvened or new meeting so as to serve notice for the Committee to obtain the necessary powers.

There was no title then of Chairman of the Committee or indeed of any sub-committee. At each meeting an ad hoc chairman was proposed to take the chair, presumably the most senior person present. This system persisted until the early '60s. Presumably the earlier method led to great consistency of policy and conduct of the affairs of the Club.

MEMBERSHIP
The membership over all of the period covered in this chapter was remarkably steady in numbers and not much less than at present. Occasional flurries of excitement arose if the number dropped by

Kilkenny Castle with
brewery transport
(see this page)

about ten but there was no difficulty in immediate restoration. The Club was always thought to be difficult to join but this was not so: it was merely selective, the Rules providing that it was a Club for gentlemen of kindred interests. The principle operated seems to have been that if some became Members who were less kindred then the operation of *similia similibus curentur* would take over as a natural course.

The Membership was certainly very wide-spread and far-reaching. The Club listed amongst its Members The Lord Chancellor, several judges and many titled people. A considerable number of the Members had been and still is drawn from the professionals, particularly the medical, legal and academic sectors. The proximity of St. Vincent's and other hospitals, as well as the Royal College of Surgeons and University College in Earlsfort Terrace, no doubt were contributory reasons for this. Another explanation for this doubtless would have been the proximity of Merrion Square, Fitzwilliam Square and similar addresses, when these were still residential areas. However, proximity was only one factor since it alone would not draw together as Members so many of kindred outlook. Many an entertaining evening was spent at the dinner table with current affairs and historical events featuring regularly. To have been a fly on the wall on some of these occasions would have been a privilege indeed.

There have been, in this period, amongst the Members, a Taoiseach; several Chief Justices and other members of the Judiciary; an artist; several professors; a Monsignor; many diplomats; some architects; more than one miller and several industrialists. Every facet of successful Dublin and provincial life was embraced by the Club.

As a policy it has been decided in this chapter to avoid mentioning names as far as possible, for to include is to exclude. However this policy is to be departed from for a brief interlude, and this will doubtless illustrate the point.

There have been several families with three brothers Members at the same time and several second generation Members sometimes overlapping and other relationships intervening. Amongst the 'multiple' Members certain names spring to mind such as Leonard, Davy, Meenan, Boydell, O'Connor-Donelan, to mention but a few; and there have often been father and son memberships concurrently, and these factors still apply, which must carry the meaning that some families regard the Club not only as traditional but also of heritage significance. After all, the Club is one hundred and fifty years old this year, and was founded 25 years after Napoleon's Battle of Waterloo.

One family, however, appears to be notable in the life of the Club and there are no records which show that this is not unique, which it must be. This is the Smithwick family of Kilkenny fame. The present member, Peter Smithwick, had a great-great grandfather believed to have been a founder Member and who was a close friend of Daniel O'Connell. He was Edmond Smithwick JP. His son John William Smithwick DL, JP was a Member. His son, in turn, James Smithwick JP was also a Member, followed by his son Walter Smithwick, a Member for many years. Thus, it seems that there was a long line of unbroken generations which must be without parallel. If there were gaps it must be through demise but not generation.

Before passing from the Membership discussion let us permit ourselves to mention but two names. Firstly Dr. Thomas A. McLaughlin (1943) who was so closely identified with the Electricity Supply Board and especially famous in connection with the Shannon Scheme for hydro-electricity for much of the country. He had served on the Committee and House Committee in his time. Secondly there was James O'Brien (1922) a country Member and State Solicitor of great personality and historical experience. He was a marvellous raconteur with an acute memory which did not stop at the Clotworthy Rowley case. More than one Member often wished that he could record the coverage at the Members' table, especially when James had moved to town, as in his retirement he was a more frequent visitor.

While it may be thought that Membership references seem a bit loaded in favour of Town Members it must be made clear that Country Members were always a fresh breeze. They enjoyed staying in the premises when matters brought them to town and though the bedrooms were perhaps a bit too like Club bedrooms they appreciated being looked after by that universally departed service in the person of a valet. The Country Members were no less distinguished than their city counterparts and were always happy to bring in the word from outside the Pale.

SUBSCRIPTION

The Club subscription around the period under review did not vary much and seems to have been about seven guineas for Town Members. The Committee spent much time considering this and entrance fees. The principle emerging seems to have been that if the number of Members dropped so might the subscription and certainly the entrance fee was dropped in such situations. Suffice it to say that as late as 1954 the Town Membership fee was £5 and the entrance fee £10.

DINING ROOM MEALS

The only record of the standard and prices of the lunches and dinners appeared some years ago when a Club Menu Book was stated to be available to the Club if it wished to make an offer for it. The Committee of the time expressed no such desire and felt that it should have been presented to the Club, which is no doubt true. It is certain that no such books have been in existence for very many years. The minutes, however, record that in the 1920s and 1930s there was a 7/6d lunch and it can be recalled that in the 1950s and 1960s there was still a 7/6d lunch; and very good it was. One can only suppose that the lunch of the earlier period must have been quite exceptional. For a comparision one has only to refer to a Jammet's menu of 1934 where a sirloin steak cost 3s and a mixed grill 2/6d. Roast pheasant was about the same. The conclusion must be that many Members partook of the Club fare *faute de mieux*.

FUNCTIONS

The main functions in the Club were, of course, the Grand National Dinner followed by an auction sweep; the Derby Dinner and the Cambridgeshire Dinner, which also had sweeps run, although it is not clear if these latter were auction sweeps. One supposes that they were. There was also a Reading Out Dinner, at which the names of any Members who had not paid their annual subscriptions were read out, unless another Member spoke for them. Advance notice, of course, was given to the relevant Members. This must have been a traumatic experience for all concerned but it did happen. The practice died out in later years although the provision was still in the Rule Book in the early 1950s.

The Grand National Dinner was probably the most important dinner in the Club over the years and it seems that the menu never changed. It is recited above.

The cost of dinner in the 1950s was one guinea, but do not forget that it included a glass of sherry and champagne throughout the dinner. This was understood to encourage the auction which followed. It was memorable to see the head waiter covering the entire room with a Jeroboam of champagne suspended from a sling across his shoulders until all were primed and plied. The dinner was subsidised out of the ticket purchase money for the sweeps, a practice later abandoned in favour of the punters. Needless to say the function was always full. There was also a tradition at this dinner that only two speeches were permitted and these were one from the member of longest standing present, and one from the member of shortest standing. The speeches were to be of shortest duration and this was always enforced. Mercifully this practice still persists.

RELATIONSHIP WITH OTHER CLUBS

The Club always enjoyed quite close relationships with other adjoining clubs on St. Stephen's Green. These appear to have been on an ad hoc basis as needs arose perhaps due to functions. There was no such thing in those days as holiday closing. Staff holidays were staggered so as to maintain the tradition of service facilities.

In 1922 it appears that the premises of the Kildare Street Club were forcibly occupied and they seem to have applied to the University Club and the Hibernian United Service Club for accommodation. The University Club asked our Club to extend similar facilities. The view of the committee was that if applied for they would certainly consider it. This happened a little later and the discussion included the fear that we might also have to face occupation. This view did not prevail and the Club extended facilities with Judge Wylie, on the committee, supporting the proposal in the terms that "it would be the sporting thing to do."

Reciprocity still survives and is much availed of as need arises. Towards the end of 1922 The Sackville Street Club was to close its doors and an arrangement was made that the Stephen's Green Club would absorb a limited number of their Members. It seems that we also acquired some of their furniture and the like, perhaps to accommodate the increased numbers.

Cartoon by Frank Reynolds presented to the Club by G.V. Martyn *(see illustration, p.95).*

PREMISES

The Club's premises are discussed elsewhere, but suffice it to say that there were various changes and additions made over the years. The premises having been a residence initially such was inevitable, and anyone who has seen copies of the earlier layout plans would appreciate these changes. The Club's Honorary Architect, Mr. W.H. Byrne, had produced a variety of plans over the years.

The most significant changes in which Members would be interested concern the present Members' Bar. This was at one time the Secretary's office. It had also been the second Billiard Room and at one stage a Member's bedroom! On the latter occasion the arrangement made was on the condition that the change would be at no cost to the Club. The Member presumably had to bear the cost of any conversion and decoration himself. This must have been one of the most commodious bedrooms in Dublin.

There was no proper bar in the Club until, perhaps, the time of the Second World War; for several of the older members often referred to the original facility which merely was a space at the end of the ground floor corridor with service from behind the glass partition which is now a store-room. Perhaps there was no real demand for change due to the full waiter service which was then provided. The old facility was affectionately referred to as 'the hole-in-the-wall.'

During each war period many of the members had to resort for transport to the bicycle and these were accommodated in the back hall passage behind the Porter's office. Trams were still the standard form of public transport and many will remember this. The arrival on the scene of the motor car began to increase and in 1928 the Committee put up a notice requesting Members not to park their motor cars in front of the Club. This is not readily understood and goodness knows how it worked out.

The splendid Reading Room on the first floor at the front of the house has always been seen as one of the finest rooms in Dublin and later members were permitted to have a *morceau* of food while enjoying the reading material. Presumably the intention was for afternoon tea.

FURNISHINGS

The Members will mostly be familiar in general with the furnishings in the Club. It may not be inopportune, nonetheless, to refer to some of them.

Firstly, there are the famous Spy cartoons in the Member's Bar. There are now 51 of these, which must constitute a unique collection. There had been 53 until recently. These were originally published in

106

book form with the covering text on the facing page. Our collection has been mounted and framed, and perhaps it is not generally known that the text is affixed to the back of each. One has only to look to see the historical references. The Members have tried to arrange a grouping of Irish connections on the fireplace wall and inter alia these include Lord Morris, the ancestor of our present Member. Also included is George Moore. Elsewhere amongst the famous is Gordon Bennett. Then we have the three three-quarter length portraits of Sir Percy Nugent, Bart., Walter Sweetman and Pierce Mahony who are believed to have been original Members. Perhaps the most striking of these is that of Sir Percy Nugent who is depicted as gazing upon his successors with penetrating eye. It would be nice to see this portrait restored to its original position gazing down on the Members' table.

The Malton prints in the bar corridor should not be overlooked. They have been shunted around latterly in a manner which may not facilitate keeping track of them, and perhaps as they were a set they should be maintained as a set in their original positions. The period in which they were acquired by the Club has not shown up in the records.

In the front hall there was the famous 'Daniel O'Connells' chair' and a pair of splendid mahogany 'wine coolers' on cupboard bases. The chair and one of the coolers were later to disappear having been 'sent out for repairs.' Neither sight nor sign has been seen of them since!

In 1927 a Member going abroad asked the committee to keep for him a mounted buffalo head, to which they agreed. No doubt this is the origin of Sambar and his compatriots who greet all entering the front hall.

As we close a study of this period it might be as well to lay to rest the variously recounted 'horse' story. The facts appear to be that late one evening, just after the war when cars were off the road, a member called for a *fiacre*. When this arrived and there was a delay in the cabbie picking up his fare he complained about missing other fares. He was offered a bottle of stout to console him and after further complaint about getting his horse back to stabling the member had two bottles of stout sent out in a basin to the horse. It was a short journey, and perhaps a slow one.

We may end this review with the hope that the best of the Club traditions may survive despite the many changes that have been brought about: *Forse che si, forse che no*.

Ballade in Honour
of His Honour Judge Davitt

The provenance of the following verses – which, it must be admitted, do some violence to the established Ballade form – is explained in the following extract from a memo from Maurice Davitt to Maurice Tempany dated 16 February 1990: '. . . when Monkstown visited Skerries some years ago for a rugby fixture I fortunately or unfortunately got into a session with Plug Flanagan. Plug told me a story which I took with a grain of salt that my old man had tried to persuade him to join the Stephen's Green Club and his refusal was set out in a poem he wrote. To prove his point he left the rugby club and returned some minutes later with the enclosed ballade. . . .'. Leo (Plug) Flanagan, in spite of his metrical protestations, became a Member of the SGC in 1957.

As a writer of the Ballade you're profound
AND YOUR HONOUR will permit me when I say
You're as fast across the squash court as a hound
And you'll listen to a lesser man, I pray
Lest you see them place my headstone on a mound
And me, in bathospheric depths below the ground:
From the Club in Stephen's Green take me away.

Now your fame all over Ireland does redound,
Host and Sportsman, Bon Viveur, if I'd my way,
Head of Ireland like King Dathi you'd be crowned
What higher tribute, Davitt, can I pay?
Once your brandy and Bob's whiskey did abound
And I drove home for hours, till quite distrait,
I gazed upon a sign four miles from Bray,
When from your Club in Stephen's Green I went away.

As a judge of vintage port you are renowned,
For I found out that again to my dismay
By the seven saints called Stephen I'll be bound
I was two months on the waggon to a day.
Now my friends are dropping drunken off the quay
And on the scatter every evening I am found,
Rather house me with the mentally unsound,
But from the Club in Stephen's Green take me away.

ENVOI
Prince, when next you put your wig on, being gowned
Pronounce this verdict, in your mercy: "Yes, O.K.,

You may put him in the nearest village pound
And from the Club in Stephen's Green lead him away"

FURTHER ENVOI
Prince of Hosts, you know I love you like a brother,
And it isn't just the question of the sub,
I have talked the whole thing over with my mother
And I dare not undertake to join your Club.

Table Talk

MARK LEONARD

Mark Leonard

From the earliest records in the Club's possession it is possible to establish the fact that the game of billiards was a favourite pastime of members. Billiards predates the game of snooker by many hundreds of years: it is now generally accepted that the latter originates from a hybrid of three games: 'Blackpool,' 'Pyramids' and 'Billiards' and was devised in Jubbulpore, India in or about 1875 by the aristocratic Colonel Sir Neville Francis Fitzgerald Chamberlain, a serving officer in the British Army. It is a matter for speculation as to whether it was to relieve the boredom of the commissioned officers stationed abroad, or to distract them from other more steamy pursuits, that the game of snooker was devised.

It is, however, unlikely that the bold Colonel could have foreseen the extent of popularity of the game today. Snooker was introduced into England in about 1885 and the modern scoring system adopted in 1891. Championship records exist for amateurs from 1916 and for professionals from 1927. The game, however, still languished in popularity far behind the game of billiards – that is until the renowned skill of Joe Davis and latterly the advent of colour television coverage of the sport, which brought the game into millions of homes. It is only fitting, before proceeding further, to refer to the infamous remark quoted by the author Duncan in his book *The Life and Letters of Herbert Spencer*: 'It was remarked to me by the Late Charles Roupell . . . . that to play billiards well was a sign of an ill-spent youth'.

From an analysis of our Club records billiards was, however, the more favoured pastime of the Members until about the mid-1920s – mention is first recorded of snooker in 1926. The extent of popularity of billiards and subsequently snooker may be gauged by the fact that the Club possessed two tables which were located in two separate designated rooms. By deduction it would appear that these rooms were the present Members' Bar and the existing Snooker Room; for in December 1874 the Committee gave its approval to the expenditure of £4.4.1 for the cleaning of billiards boxes in the West Room and £2.6.10 in the East Room. Expenditure approved by Committee and House Committees generally consisted of the purchase of new sets of billiard balls. Historically this equipment was made from ivory and it was generally accepted that it was possible to make five billiard balls from the tusk of a mature elephant. Thankfully today the equipment is manufactured from Crystalate as new sets of billiards balls were purchased at a yearly frequency. It is worth recording that this commodity did not come cheaply, for in April 1893, for example, a set was ordered at an approved cost of £4.4.0.

The Club records testify that since before the end of the last century amongst the general staff engaged was an appointed Billiard Marker. This member of staff was obviously highly valued by the Members as witnessed by the distribution of the then traditional Christmas Bonus to staff members. It is recorded for example that in 1896 the Billiard Marker M. Fallon, then with seven years of service, was allocated by the Committee the sum of £8:10:0 out of a total collection of £93 shared between 16 Staff Members. His annual wages are recorded as being £30.

A major expenditure was authorized by the Committee in 1896 whereby the sum of £35 for improvements to the billiard table was sanctioned. Notwithstanding this expenditure, however, it took from March 1897 until October 1899 for the Committee to agree upon the best method of providing electric light to the Billiard Rooms! This decision was taken after the appointment of a Sub-Committee, consisting of Messrs George Fottrell, J E Martin and Pierce Nolan who were instructed to inspect the billiard rooms of hotels where electric lighting had been installed. Following submission of their report it was resolved to authorize the Sub-Committee to carry out the work in the best manner possible for a sum not exceeding £25.0.0.

In 1902 the Committee ordered that amongst the Servants' duties (7 in total) that 'Two waiters shall always be in attendance on the Billiard, Smoking, Strangers' and Reading Rooms, both in the afternoon and after dinner'. In November 1902, a Club Member, John Meldon, wrote to the Committee suggesting that they should arrange for an exhibition match of billiards between professionals. After discussion the Secretary was to inform Mr Meldon that the Committee did not think it desirable to do so, in the interests of elder Members who might be inconvenienced thereby.

The Members' interest in billiards was substantial. In March 1908, a 'memorial' was presented by Leo Plunkett to the Committee acting on behalf of Members who wished to obtain a standard billiard table for the Club. The memorandum appears to have stated that 'Subscriptions in Aid' would be given by Members and that the cost to the Club would not exceed £40. This proposal appears to have met with the Committee's approval but seems to have been modified later that month by the proposal to expend £30 on conversion of the table to a standard pattern. In June 1909 the Committee decided to procure electric bell indicators which were to be erected outside the Smoking, Billiard and Card Rooms. In March 1913 Dr Horne proposed and Dr Dempsey seconded the following resolution to the General Committee 'That the Billiard Table at present used for the Amateur Championships of Ireland be purchased for a sum not exceeding Sixty Five Guineas (provided that a minimum sum of £50 be placed at the disposal of the Committee) and that the House Committee be empowered to negotiate with J. Duncan as to his accepting the position of Billiard Marker to the Club'. This resolution was unanimously adopted. The following May Dr Dempsey and Leo Plunkett proposed and seconded that 'A Member receiving a lesson from the Billiard Professional, between the hours of 10.00 am and 1.30 pm is entitled to the exclusive use of the new Billiard Room for the time being. The tariff for lessons will be found posted in each room'. This proposal was also unanimously passed. In February 1914 the Committee favoured the continuance of the engagement of J. Duncan, Billiard Professional for a further period of six months. In the Annual Report for 1913, presented to the Members in February 1914, it is recorded that shortly after the Last Annual General Meeting a new billiard table was presented to the Club by certain Members at whose suggestion the experiment was made of engaging a billiard professional for one year.

In November 1916 the Honorary Secretary introduced the subject of a proposal to the Committee to hold an Inter-Alia Billiard Handicap which some Members had expressed to him a desire to have inaugurated. After discussion it was proposed and seconded by Dr Dempsey and Lane Joynt 'That an Inter-Club Billiard Handicap be held with the object of assisting the funds of the Red Cross Organisation, and that the Members of the University and United Service Club be invited to participate, the whole assist of Entry money to be devoted to the object mentioned'. On a division, six voted in favour and four against and the motion was declared carried. It is thought likely that this decision was the start of what has become traditionally one of the Stephen's Green Club's annual fixtures, namely our friendly match in snooker with The Hibernian United Services Club held every year in early Spring. Reference is made once to a fixture match in 1979 at the invitation of Fitzwilliam Lawn Tennis Club. In this context it is also worthwhile recording the autumnal event inaugurated in 1989 with the Royal St George Yacht Club.

St. Stephen's Green 1797. This well-known drawing by James Malton shows the John Van Nost statue of King George II which the Corporation of Dublin erected in 1753. It also illustrates the point that we had a few four-legged residents 'On the Green' before the arrival of the 'Whigs'.

The Earl of Mulgrave. Constantine Henry Phipps, M.P. (Later Marquis of Normanby) was a popular Liberal Viceroy during the formative years 1835/39. He was previously Governor of Jamaica which may explain the little black boy. This portrait by Nicholas J. Crowley is at the National Gallery.

The Earl of Milltown. Joseph Leeson and his family were ground landlords of Number 9, St. Stephen's Green for some two hundred years. This fine portrait by Anthony Lee also hangs at the National Gallery.

Peter La Touche of Belview and Luggala, Co. Wicklow. As a banker, he acquired No. 9, St. Stephen's Green in 1812. This portrait – 'Gentleman with Gun and Dog by Robert Hunter' – is another contribution from the National Gallery.

Lafranchini on the landing. In his contribution to our history Austin Dunphy tells us that 'The rococo work in the St. Stephen's Green Club is generally regarded as amongst the finest in Dublin and is of European importance'.

The Great Staircase. The same contributor describes this club treasure, which dates from about 1756, as 'One of the most beautiful timber staircases in Ireland'.

Comfort in the Card Room. The warm glow of a good coal fire framed by the beautiful Chinese Chippendale chimneypiece is a most welcoming sight in the Card Room.

... and comfort in the bedroom. Work on the first of the recently refurbished en-suite bedrooms was completed in 1989 and members may look forward to increased comforts in this area as the programme continues.

The Dining Room – Pictured in all its splendour prior to our Sesquicentennial Luncheon on Monday 9th July when The President of Ireland, His Excellency Dr. Patrick Hillery, was Guest of Honour.

The Reading Room.
Thanks to the generosity of two longstanding members it was possible to celebrate our Sesquicentennial by restoring completely the reading room and its exquisite plasterwork ceilings so that future generations may continue to enjoy an uninterrupted aspect to St. Stephen's Green from these magnificent surroundings.

The Drawing Room.
A copy of one of the beautiful Lafranchini works from Riverstown House, Co. Cork – a panel depicting 'Grammer' c.1740 – was included as part of the Drawing Room refurbishment completed in 1988.

The Club Trustees Cornelius
F. Smith, James J. Davy,
Patrick J. Brennan

The General Committee (Back l. to r.) Michael Nugent, Jerry Corry, Philip O'Connor,
Derek Davy (Hon. Treasurer), Antony Leonard, John O'Driscoll, Pat Kilbride.
(Front l. to r.) Desmond O'Neill (Hon. Sec.), David Callaghan (Vice-Chairman), Brian Price
(Chairman), Austin Dunphy, John Hedigan. Other committee members missing from this
photograph are included overleaf.

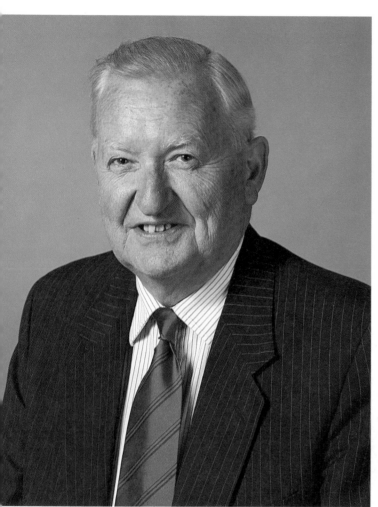

OUR CURRENT CHAIRMAN

"I am looking forward to reading this history. I believe we will learn for the first time how the club has developed and, perhaps more important, a marker is being planted for the future. We are grateful to the literary explorers".

Brian Price
Eze-sur-mer. 6-9-90.

Missing from the photograph of our General Committee on the previous page are (top right) Tom Hannigan, (lower left) Tony Walsh and (lower right) Harry Hannon.

January 1923 saw the first appointment of The Billiards Sub-Committee which consisted of Leo Plunkett, John McCann, Daniel Gillman and Henry Campbell who were proposed and seconded by Lord Justice O'Connor and Sir George Fottrell. This Sub-Committee served until October 1924, when they were replaced by the following: Mr Martin, George Murphy (later Sir George Murphy Bart), St. J. Considine and Dr R. White. Since that period, the following Members have served on the Billiards and/or Snooker Sub-Committee: A. Lloyd Blood; Capt. Horne, N. Manly, T.A. Brindley, J.H. Browning; F.W. Browning; P.D. Matthews; B.P. Matthews; N.G. Downes; C.C. Callaghan; W. Lennox; B. Wellwood; J.D. Hackett; T.R.G. Wall; J.P. Doyle; H. Hamilton; E.M. Murphy; R. Cuddy; V.F.J. Kelly; P. Butler; R.T. Whelan; J.F. Bolger; Preston Doyle; D.H. O'Neill; B.J. Matthews; M. Tempany; P.J. Brennan; J.A. Short; C. Myerscough; P. Fanning; C.G.

Cartoon by Frank Reynolds *(see illustration, p.105)*.

Smith; M.W. Leonard; Peter Doyle; D. McGing; P. Murphy; B. Brindley; M.P. Fitzpatrick; P. Lyons; D. Anderson.

In February 1928 the General Committee received a letter signed by 24 members of the Club suggesting that the little-used Billiard Room be converted into a Bar Lounge. A special Sub-Committee reported back to the General Committee in March 1928 and following discussion it was generally agreed to utilise the Second Billiard Room as a Lounge. The Committee decided to advertise the billiard table and surplus equipment for sale at a minimum price of £80. Whilst two replies were received to the advertisement, no sale resulted, and it was ultimately decided to dispose of the items to a William Hayes for the sum of £25. In December 1928 the Committee decided to use the vacated Second Billiard Room as the Secretary's office.

It would appear that the Club arranged for exhibition billiard matches on a fairly frequent basis over the intervening period, for even in February 1950 the Honorary Secretary was directed to write to Nicholas Manly to express the deepest gratitude of the Committee for his efforts in organising such events. Billiards appears to have been the principal activity until about 1926 when snooker appears to have taken priority. Our records clearly identify that a Snooker Handicap Auction was held in 1926.

In January 1956 E.L. Crosby announced that the Honourable Mr Justice Wylie had kindly presented a cup for the Club Snooker Competition. The Committee accepted this gift with grateful thanks. The donor of the cup suggested that T.A. Doyle, who had won the recent Snooker Competition, should have his name inscribed on the cup. As all Members know, this tournament is played for every Autumn and appended herewith is The Roll of Honour. It is perhaps fitting to record the contribution made by the Honourable Mr Justice Wylie to all the activities of the Club. He loved a frame of snooker and frequently played at lunchtime. All are indebted to him. Apart from the generosity of those Members who subscribed towards the purchase cost of our fine table and the gift by Judge Wylie, there is mention in our records of the presentation of a painting in October 1966 by D. Fitzgerald, which was to be hung in the Billiard Room. Unfortunately it no longer hangs there. Instead there is an amusing caricature sketch presented by G.V. Martyn. It is strange to relate but in November 1961 Dr McLaughlin suggested to the Committee that notices be displayed to remind Members that a guest may only be introduced into the Billiard Room provided that he is lunching or dining in the Club with the introducing Member. The background to this suggestion is not recounted in the Club's annals but it may just be a sufficient reminder to recall the story contained in our records whereby in 1976 the then Chairman of the General Committee reported of the finding of the wife of a Member with her husband and some other Members and Guests after midnight, no less, in the Snooker Room in flagrant breach of our Bye-laws.

It is only fitting to record that the Billiard or Snooker Room invariably throughout our existence imposed charges upon Members for its use. Regrettably our records do not identify in full the extent of these charges except for the following: the House Committee at its meeting in June 1953 decided on the introduction of a charge similar to that in the Billiards Room of 1/– per head per game for billiards played in the afternoon and a charge of 2/– per game after 7.00 pm. In April 1962 the Club price per frame was to be increased from 1/- to 1/6d before Dinner and from 2/– to 2/6d after dinner. Historically it is worth noting that these charges in various amounts continued to operate until about 1980 when the Committee decided that the Add-On cost involved in keeping tabulations and records of the amounts collected twice daily from the cash box was no longer justifiable. To give Members an indication of the popularity of billiards and snooker and the use of these activities within the Club it is perhaps fitting to quote the following extracts from our Club accounts:

		£.	s.	d.
1914:	Received from Games played	136	19	9
	Expended on Table	21	7	7
	Profit	**115**	**12**	**2**
1925:	Received from Games	151	8	0
	Expended	17	2	3
	Profit	**134**	**5**	**9**

Whether the charge be six pence or a shilling per frame per Member it can readily be calculated that considerable use was made of these facilities.

Traditionally it would appear that the Stephen's Green Club successfully ran Auction Sweeps on Billiards and Snooker Tournaments. Apart from the Sweep Prize, a financial prize was given to the respective Tournament Winners – that is, until the advent of the Wylie Cup; and latterly the decision to present a Waterford cut glass tankard inscribed with the Club motif to the individual winner of the Wylie Cup or the snooker foursomes. In regard to this decision, particular thanks should be recorded to Michael P. Fitzpatrick and Basil Brindley.

Currently, with our two major snooker tournaments held in the Spring and Autumn of every year, the game is encouraged by recent sub-committees on a daily basis. All are welcome to play and furthermore to participate in the Special Classic session, kindly arranged by M.P. Fitzpatrick, one evening per week in the Spring and Autumn. In 1983, following his victory in The Wylie Cup, Des Fitzgerald kindly presented a timber-framed plaque to accommodate the names of further winners of this tournament.

In so far as it is possible to obtain from our Records the Snooker Roll of Honour is as follows:

		Date Joined SGC	Service as Hon Officer or Committee
1924	Dr Thomas Considine.	1904	
1926	Capt. Francis Horne.	1922	Hon. Secretary
do	Major Anson Maher.	1919	
1927	Cecil Briscoe.	1914	
1930	Leo Plunkett.	1919	
1950	Kevin Mulcahy.	1946	

THE WYLIE CUP

1955	Doyle, Thomas A.	1943	Judge, Trustee
1956	Threlfall, Bill	1947	
1957	Lambert, Eric	1948	
1958	Hannin, Thomas	1938	
1959	Browning, Jackie	1944	
1960	Matthews, Brian P.	1951	
1961	Hodson, Stephen	1949	
1962	McCarthy, Willie	1950	
1963	Lennox, Bill	1949	
1964	Walsh, Anthony	1964	
1965	Threlfall, Bill	1947	Twice winner
1966	Murphy, Major Eddie	1950	
1967	Winston, Martin P.	1960	
1968	Wall, Tom	1949	
1969	McGovern, Conn	1952	
1970	Matthews, Brian P.	1951	
1971	Hamilton, Hugh	1962	
1972	Matthews, Brendan J.	1948	
1973	Downes, Cola	1944	
1974	Bolger, John	1963	
1975	Kelly, Vincent	1969	
1976	Dunne, Dr. John	1937	Competed since 1948, twice winner
1977	Matthews, Brendan J.	1948	Twice winner
1978	Carr, Joseph B.	1961	

1979	Short, Jim	1969	
1980	Whelan, Ronald T.	1970	
1981	Pigot, David R.	1953	
1982	Fitzgerald, Desmond	1963	
1983	Matthews, Brian P.	1951	Third time winner
1984	Higgins, Niall	1952	
1985	Dunne, Dr. John	1937	Twice winner
1986	Lyons, Peter	1986	
1987	Leonard, Mark	1976	
1988	Riordan, Bill	1980	
1989	Lennon, Declan	1970	

A new competition this year (1990): The Stephen's Green Club Sesquicentennial Snooker Champions & Maidens, was won by Desmond O'Neill.

The Club, Cricket and the American Connection

DAVID R. PIGOT

David R. Pigot

Anyone who knows the immediate past Chairman of the Club will sympathise and forgive me for having the temerity to proffer this contribution: So eloquent is Basil, it was extremely difficult to refuse him, particularly when he pointed out (regrettably with some truth) that I had done little or nothing for the Club in over 30 years and as I was entering my (mark you, not the) 90s, it was about time I did!

My first reaction was that it would be difficult to find many Members of the Club who had played cricket at any meaningful level. With the help of Neil Smith (without which this simply could not have been written), to my very pleasant surprise I discovered that there are, in fact, quite a number of them.

Some of those Members lived in more leisured times than we enjoy today and, as well as playing a considerable amount of first class cricket, were able to find the lengthy time then required to sail to the North American continent with the All Ireland teams in 1888 and 1892. They included J.M. Meldon, the Australian-born brothers E.R. and J.P. Fitzgerald (the former arguably the best amateur wicket-keeper of his day) and W. Synott, all of whom were with the 1888 party. Meldon was indeed (although only 23) captain of the 1892 team of which T. Considine was also a member.

It was Meldon who, inevitably, lost a 'toss' with the great W.G. Grace who had called 'woman', the coin having Britannia on one side and Queen Victoria on the other! However, Andrew D. Comyn re-dressed the balance in 1902, appealing from the boundary with such vigour that the umpire gave the great man out despite his protestation that it was only the noise of his 'squeaky bat'. In the case of W.G. the boot was usually on the other foot! G.J. Meldon, the following year, also made a century against Grace's London County XI, a very strong team. There is indeed little doubt but that W.G. graced our Club in person, an acknowledgment of an invitation to do so appearing in the Club records.

118

Other distinguished cricketers who were also members of the Club were D.F. Gillman (who was responsible for many first class teams visiting Ireland in the early 1900s and initiating the annual match against Scotland), and some other members of the Meldon family, Thomas, Albert, Joseph and Louis A. Also members were Harry Reade, who played cricket and rugby for Ireland, forming (with Dickie Lloyd) a famous half back partnership, and Walter Pigot, grandson of a Founder Member, who played for Trinity in 1910 and was capped for Ireland at hockey. Of more recent vintage were George McVeagh, a quadruple international (hockey, tennis, squash, and cricket) who made 100 against the West Indies and took four catches in College Park in 1928 in a famous victory, and N.H. (Ham) Lambert, who played for Ireland before and after the Second World War and was an international rugby referee. Whether the Club was represented on the first American tour in 1879, or on the 1909 Tour, I am unaware, but two

Alan Mooney leading the Club XI onto the field at Pembroke Cricket Club, 1944. Cahir Davitt is third in line. *(Photo: Tony Brindley).*

119

other members (Pat Dineen and your scribe – a great-great grandson of a Founder Member) travelled with the most recent touring team to the United States and Canada in 1973. Both had played in the nine wicket defeat of the West Indies at Sion Mills in 1969 when they were bowled out for 25, their lowest score against anyone anywhere anytime.

Many of the Club's present members played Senior Cricket with distinction, including Reggie Jackson, Brendan McGrath, Kevin O'Riordan, Cyril Irwin and Maurice Curran, to mention but a few.

History does not reveal whether the Club boasted its own XI in days gone by. We do, however, know that it fielded a team at Pembroke C.C. as long ago as 1944 under the captaincy of Alan Murray (after whom one of the Leinster Senior Trophies is named) and, more recently, thanks to the enthusiasm of Pat Kilbride, matches were played against The Armagh Club in 1987, 1988 and 1989. In this the Club's sesquicentennial year as well as the annual match against the Armagh Club a fixture with the Phoenix Cricket Club may be arranged. Many of those I have mentioned from the early years were prominent members of Phoenix (which celebrated its own sesquincentennial year in 1980) and many others today including Michael Kennedy, Pascal Butler, Desmond O'Neill, Paul Fanning and others are loyal (if occasionally masochistic) supporters.

The idea of the Stephen's Green Club playing an annual cricket match (perhaps against its next door neighbour) in St. Stephen's Green itself is undoubtedly a thought to conjure with. Unhappily, I doubt if it is one that will ever catch on – there would be too many ducks!

'When I was a Lad . . .' 1945–1990

MAURICE TEMPANY

"It is a very curious thing", said Joseph Chamberlain in an after-dinner speech reported in *The Times* on 21 March 1892: "that the types of the House of Commons are constant, although the men change". He stated further: "I have never known the House of Commons without a funny man. (Laughter). When he dies . . . there is another immediately to take his place. He is a man with a natural taste for buffoonery . . . Then there is the House of Commons bore – of course there is more than one (Laughter). He is generally a man who is very clever, a man of encyclopaedic information . . .".

Maurice Tempany

Much of this could well be applied to the Stephen's Green Club: in many such ways does it bear resemblance to the House of Commons. I am not suggesting for one minute that our Chairman equates with the Prime Minister but it is true to say that the hallowed traditions of the Club have been preserved to a significant degree by successive Chairmen and committees. It is certainly true to say that over the years the Club has had its share of funny men and also perhaps a greater share of Club bores. Many members will recall those interesting after-dinner sessions when eleven Members were selected to 'play' against eleven Fitzwilliam Lawn Tennis Club members having similar soporific conversational skills!

The author of this chapter first became acquainted with the Club in the autumn of 1948 when, as an Articled Clerk (now called Trainee) in the firm of Thomas Geoghegan and Company, Chartered Accountants, 4 College Green, Dublin, who were the Club auditors, he had the good fortune to be allotted to assisting at the quarterly audits. The benefits of enjoying a luncheon each day at no charge represented a considerable cash saving and a significant gastronomic education for someone who had just completed seven years' boarding school education in County Kildare during World War II. The consideration shown to a raw youth by seemingly extremely elderly Members who

121

visited the office was quite extraordinary. There was a pervasive atmosphere of peacefulness and calm – no sign then of the modern trend of meeting deadlines with mandatory overtime working! The daily stint for that Articled Clerk was 10 am to 1 pm and 2.30 to 5 on Monday to Friday and 10 am to 1 pm on Saturday.

An indication of the general state of affairs of the Club in the early 1950s can be gleaned from the minutes of the Annual General Meeting held on Monday 12 March 1951. The first thing to be observed is that it was held at 5 pm and attracted 72 members compared with 22 at the AGM of the previous year. The members present appear to have represented quite a wide spectrum of the business and professional men of the time. There are no less than 12 medical doctors designated in the attendance list with seven stockbrokers hard on their heels but not a sign of a chartered accountant – and just two insurance brokers. At that stage the Club's assets were valued at about £19,000, funded by accumulated surpluses amounting to £5,500 together with Club debentures of £3,000, bank overdraft of £7,000 and the rest from creditors. The meeting was facing a deficit for the year of £53!

Cahir Davitt

Thomas Geoghegan, the Club's first auditor and the author's first employer.
(*Institute of Chartered Accountants of Ireland*)

The extraordinary thing about the minutes is that while they record a debate as to whether the annual subscription should be increased to £15 and the entrance fee to £20 there is no record of the actual outcome of the vote – if one was taken. It is necessary to push on to 29 October 1951 when an Extraordinary General Meeting was held with 81 members attending to see that a proposal to increase the subscription from £12 to 15 guineas was tabled. Apparently the Club was faced with a deficit of £1500 for the nine months to 3 September and the resolution to increase the subscription was passed unanimously. The life subscription was also increased at that meeting from £100 to £150.

An overall review of the financial affairs of the Club in the 48 years to 1989 indicates that successive General Committees have, by and large, adopted a similar strategy. The overriding impression is that the annual subscription levels were determined with a short-term rather than a long-term focus, resulting in the frequent recurrence of relatively small annual deficits interspersed with a number of substantial deficits followed by a few years of surplus. The practice of writing-off almost every conceivable item of capital expenditure annually was the accepted accounting policy until the early 1980s when, it would seem, absolute necessity caused committees to embark on significant expenditures of a capital nature.

At that Extraordinary General Meeting on 29 October 1951 there was a spirited debate on the resolution to admit guests to the

123

Michael Kennedy (1), and David Mahony, two long-serving Honorary Secretaries and great Club characters.

Members' Bar. Walter Callan was against the proposal and pointed out 'that even if guests were excluded, as at present, the bar is uncomfortably crowded between the hours of 6.30 and 7 pm'. The resolution was defeated: 40 against to 35 in favour. The attendance included Vincent Davy, James Davy, Dr Paddy Meenan, Dr John Lanigan and John Tunney. Cahir Davitt, then President of the High Court, took the chair. Total membership at that time was about 540 (581 in 1989) and there was a buoyant demand, evidenced by the existence of a waiting list on which names were placed 'to enable members to make enquiries'. At a meeting of the General Committee on 29 January 1952 the Honorary Secretary mentions that two Members of long standing had tended their resignations and 'he understood that it was the view of the Committee that they should be elected to Honorary Life Membership. After discussion it was decided that this should not be done'.

Elections in the early 1950s were clearly a matter of great excitement and contention. The application of the Rules (no. 5(E) being relevant) revolves around the utilisation of what is called the blackball where one vote in six was sufficient to disqualify an applicant from membership. In January 1954, although the enthusiasm was high – as demonstrated by the fact that 13 candidates were approved for election – there was also a financial crisis. The catering accounts showed a loss of nearly £500 and a variety of remedies were discussed. One member thought that 'an effective economy would be to serve smaller helpings and further portions could be served to members desiring same'. Another stated that he had learned that food was being taken from the Club whilst other expense aspects considered were the high cost of light and heat and the maintenance of staff. These concerns caused the Committee to defer a programme of general repairs and renewals. Subsequently it was decided to initiate a Repairs and Improvements fund which would be funded by a Sweepstake, in which first prize was to be life membership of the Club, second prize, four years' free Membership and third prize two years' free Membership.

Records in the 1950s suggest that a large number of Members were individually concerned with the activities within the Club and the bringing in of more activity. On 26 June 1951 it was agreed that the usual facilities of Honorary Membership should be extended to officers and members of the army jumping teams competing at the Dublin Horse Show. It was also agreed that members of a South African cricket XI should be made Honorary Members during their tour in Ireland. In 1952 a General Committee was appraised of the fact that a conference of the Irish and British Medical Associations would be held in Dublin during the month of July and that a request had been received that certain doctors attending should be made Temporary Members of the Club. This was agreed, subject to their being nominated in the ordinary way. This tends to suggest that the Club held an important position in the daily lives of its Members and that they wished to share its value with visiting colleagues.

It seems evident that in the early 1950s Members were accustomed to staying overnight to a greater extent than currently. A number appear to have enjoyed the equivalent of permanent occupation of certain rooms and the minutes of the General Committee in November 1952 record that one particular Member requested permission to occupy No. 4 bedroom and to carry out certain decorations to that room. The Honorary Secretary was directed to inform him that the Committee was agreeable to his occupying the room, subject to the rules and regulations of the Club, and that, in the opinion of the Secretary he was not likely to be disturbed at short notice. Evidently the cost of redecorating the room to his own taste did not deter that Member from paying the going rate for exclusive occupation. He happened to be a Trustee of the Club and was much revered and respected during his lifetime.

In general the occupancy of the ten bedrooms of the Club remained fairly low in the priority of successive committees: indeed in the early 1950s one committee questioned their viability. The heating was by coin-operated gas fires which, by reason of the size of the rooms, was reckoned to be somewhat inadequate, especially on the colder winter nights. More than one Annual General Meeting heard impassioned

MIS EN BOUTEILLES AU CHÂTEAU POUR

The Stephen's Green Club
SESQUICENTENNIAL CELEBRATIONS

CHÂTEAU
Saint Estèphe
CRU BOURGEOIS

SAINT ESTÈPHE
APPELLATION SAINT-ESTÈPHE CONTR

12% vol.

1986

S.A.R.L. A
CHÂTEAUX S¹ ES
33250 SAIN

FRANCE

PRODUCE OF FRANCE

Saint-Véran
APPELLATION SAINT-VÉRAN CONTRÔLÉE
MIS EN BOUTEILLES POUR
The Stephen's Green Club
SESQUICENTENNIAL CELEBRATIONS
PAR

12.5% vol.

MOMMESSIN

75 cl

Les Vins Mommessin à La Grange Saint-Pierre, Mâcon, France

CHATEAU
FONTMURE
Montagne-Saint-Émilion
Appelation Montagne-Saint-Émilion Contrôlée
1985
J.FOURGEAUD
propriétaire à Montagne Gironde
PRODUCE OF FRANCE

750ml e

12%vol.

MIS EN BOUTEILLES POUR
The Stephen's Green Club
SESQUICENTENNIAL CELEBRATIONS
PAR GILBEY DE LOUDENNE
NÉGOCIANT A SAINT-ŸZANS-DE-MÉDOC GIRONDE

Special Sesquicentennial
bottlings

and eloquent pleas from Country Members for money to be spent on these rooms and the provision of bathrooms en suite. In the last decade committees have upgraded three bedrooms by the provision of bathrooms, but much more is yet to be done.

In the aftermath of World War II the Department of Health was active pursuant to the provision of the Food Regulations 1951. The Honorary Secretary of that year (then a young barrister and subsequently a High Court judge) recorded that 'the matter had been previously considered and that the Committee took the view that these regulations were not applicable to the Club'. A meeting held earlier in the same month had referred to urgent work requiring to be done with the Club cellars and the blocking off of an old sewer close to the Club premises. One can only speculate that there was some feeling that the kitchens were not in good order.

The kitchens then, as now, were situated in the basement. Early morning deliveries of groceries, milk, meat and the like were brought into the Club premises by way of the external staircase in front of the present building. A dumb waiter was used to transport cold trays, etc. to the Coffee Room which was situated in an area now occupied by the Members' Private Dining Room on the ground floor. The office of the Secretary/Manager was situated directly opposite the Coffee Room resulting in a very close relationship between the kitchen and serving staff and the office staff; indeed all endeavours within the Club were organised from these two rooms.

The Bar goods deliveries were effected largely through the laneway off Dawson Street near the RIAC, access being gained to the cellar by way of a corridor which ran on the right hand side of the present hall door directly alongside the existing office to the back of the premises to the old dispense bar which still remains, though unused. There was a hatch between the dispense bar and the office of the Secretary/ Manager and through this the daily records of bar goods sold were passed into the office for billing out, whilst Goods Received notes and

The Stephen's Green Club
9 St. Stephen's Green
Dublin 2

Nice to know you're coming along to
Our Sesquicentennial Night at the Opera

Tickets 'specially for you

Black ✕ Tie
6.00 pm Reception in Card Room
7.15 pm Gaiety Theatre
10.30 pm Buffet Supper in Club.

Secretary Telephone

the like were also submitted for the recording of purchases. From this
it will be noted that the location of the office of the Secretary/
Manager was pivotal to the general operation of the Club and was
occupied daily by the Manager and two clerks. The Housekeeper,
Headwaiter, Night Porter and the Valet all called to that office daily
to give a resumé of the previous day's goings-on and of matters which
required the attention of the Manager or his staff. I remember very
clearly listening with awesome wonder to the reports of Mrs O'Connor
the housekeeper; Michael, the Valet; the Cassidy brothers – Head
Waiter (Joe) and Wine Waiter (Michael) – all of whom added a little
spice to the otherwise boring documentation that passed through the
office for processing.

In the early 1950s many of the General Committee and House
Committee were also daily callers to that office for the purpose of
discussing matters of particular moment. These would range from
bridge matches to the annual billiard and snooker tournaments. There
were also the committees dealing with the Grand National and Derby
Sweeps to be catered for, whilst the Wine Committee and Library
Committee representatives also called at fairly frequent intervals.
There were some nine committees or sub-committees extant in 1950.
From the Manager's office also each day all catering suppliers were
spoken to by telephone and the menus for lunch and dinner were
composed and typed. I seem to recollect some hilarity at the determination of the appropriate French nomenclature to be employed for
the dinner menu. This recollection is supported by a reference in a
General Committee meeting minute in which the suggestion was
made that as the Club no longer had a French chef there was no
reason why the dinner menu should be written in French! Certain
vociferous members were not familiar with the words employed by
the Manager and chef.

The Manager's flat, adjacent to the squash court, is composed of a
drawing room, two bedrooms and a bathroom, with the upper floors
allocated to more senior staff members. This was an amenity which
the Club was able to offer at a time when its cash resources did not
permit it to pay a significant monetary reward. In the 1940s catering
management was in its infancy with the training college in Cathal
Brugha Street being almost exclusively patronised by females whilst
their male counterparts worked as assistant managers to the legendary
Toddie O'Sullivan in the Gresham Hotel. The Club itself was
fortunate in that the 1940s saw Brendan O'Regan spending a year or
two as Manager before his career took off with his hugely successful
endeavours at Shannon. It is a pleasure to record that he subsequently
became a Member of the Club and was most generous with his time
and advice to successive committees.

A sinister line in the minutes indicates that a Special General meeting was to be held on 22 December 1953 and that the views of Members would be sought as to the advisability of altering the rules regarding the admission of ladies to the Club. The deficit for the year ended 31 December 1953 was £322, and the finances were occupying the Committee's time to a considerable extent. One of the solutions was to permit lady guests to be invited to the Club to partake of refreshments within certain limited hours, without the necessity of lunching of dining. One Committee member (Dr Fitzsimons) 'was against the proposal'. He stated that ladies might remain in the Club until a late hour with a possibility of unpleasantness or humiliation. The proposal was defeated with 12 votes in favour of the proposed alteration and 28 against'. At the Annual General Meeting of 1957 the question was again put forward and on this occasion it was approved, with 22 members in favour and 4 against.

Brendan O'Regan, subsequently Chairman of Shannon Free Airport Development Co. and Bord Failte

The Club premises are a composition of many disunited areas and have been subjected to ad hoc tinkerings by way of refurbishment due to the lack of sufficient finance to complete any master plan. The external facade, for this reason, has not been materially altered in the years since the period of our review, but the lack of resources did have an impact on the buildings at the rear of the site.

The Squash Court is housed in a building separate from the main premises at the Dawson Street side of the site. Adjacent to it there is a small building in which all Club laundry work was carried out. It was then the practice of the Club until well after World War II to cover the tables with linen cloths which were removed at the coffee stage of each meal. Bedroom usage was quite high and as a consequence the laundry was a busy place with permanent regular staff employed. This work is now done on one day a week in the same building with the aid of modern equipment.

The room opposite the then Secretary's office was a source of tea and coffee but was also a resting place for staff who were on duty. There was always a hive of activity in the area of that back hall which reflected that of the Club: Members' arrivals and departures were quickly reported and all staff disciplinary matters were dealt with expeditiously. All serving staff wore uniforms and the discipline, from Hall Porter to Night Porter, was strict. The latter had a cupboard in which he held liquor for sale to members after the Bar had closed. The system in force required the Night Porter to collect a fine from each member who stayed on in the Club after midnight: there was a progressive rate of fine depending on the lateness of the hour. Fine dockets were issued and the proceeds retained in a tin box until the following day. The brand of whiskey retained by the Night Porters is the subject of many references in the minute books and it seems that

Jameson was the preferred potion of at least one Member whose name appears in the Suggestions Book – which was heavily used at that time to communicate what effectively were Members' complaints. In June 1950 it was agreed that three Suggestions Books should be provided – one in the Reading Room, one in the Members' Bar and one in the Card Room.

The entries in the Card Room book indicate a healthy level of rapport between the ordinary Member and the House Committee. In January 1964 one wrote: 'On the night of January 9 the Card room was re-opened to play. There was no gas in either of the heaters and no coal in the bucket. There was also no poker. This is a very cold room and I would request that something be done to ensure that every effort is made to provide heat'. The Secretary of the day responded with a note: 'matter has been brought to the notice of the Manageress. Explained by her that the inconveniences caused on the night in question were due to the sudden and unannounced return of the Members to the Card Room from the Strangers' Bar/Lounge where they were temporarily located'.

Another comment of a more technical nature occurs in 1967 when a Member wrote: 'Would the card committee please give a ruling on the following point with respect to a game of poker. If a player opens a pot without a sufficient hand in a game of poker (e.g. in an Ace for openers on a pair of Kings) what is the rule – should the hand be played out, and one player exposes a hand stronger than the opener, i.e. a pair of Aces or better?' The Secretary noted on 6 June 1967: 'Being referred to Cards committee'. On 15 September the original querist wrote in the book: 'How about a ruling?'

It is evident that the finances in the early 1950s were consistently scarce as a Life Membership sweepstake in April 1954 raised some £750 for the purposes of general repairs to the premises. Again in 1955 a sweepstake was held to raise more funds for the repairs and renewal fund. On that occasion the prize was a portrait to be painted by a Member, Leo Whelan RHA, the winner being entitled to designate the sitter. Leo Whelan undertook to carry out the commission for the sum of £100. This practice of funding significant expenditure from the proceeds of sweepstakes was repeated on a number of occasions. In the minutes of the General Committee of 28 May 1963 it is recorded that the Club Membership sweep would take place at 6.00 pm on 7 June, 'notices to this effect to be posted in the Club. Messrs Griffin Lynch & Company, Auditors [who replaced Thomas Geoghegan & Co in March 1960] to conduct and arrange method of draw'. It is the writer's recollection that he represented the auditors on that occasion and drew the name of the late T. P. Brindley as the winner who became entitled to Membership for life at no cost. He enjoyed his success hugely.

The front hall of the Club has been little altered over the years. The author was somewhat perturbed in the mid-sixties when entering with an eminent accountant from New York who said that he liked dining at the Stephen's Green Club as it was such a homely place with none of the glass and stainless steel of the characterless hotels around the world. "I see", he said, "that the crack in the paintwork in the hall is there since you kindly entertained me here a year ago". Such is the homeliness of our Club.

The Members' Bar and Visitors' Bar have occupied quite an amount of committee time in regard to their furniture and decor. The writer recalls a very contentious debate occurring at the time when the latter was redecorated. The late Leo Whelan, RHA, kindly presented to the Club a painting of a reclining female lady in a state of undress. It appears that this caused some distress to certain Members as a consequence of which the artist was required to repaint certain areas before it was hung. Access to the Members' Bar was a jealously-guarded prerogative, Members being frequently reminded of the necessity to prevent guests from paying for drinks and of the requirement that only visitors dining with Members were permitted access before dinner.

The preservation of the Snooker Room for use by Members only was also a matter of some considerable determination by various committees. One rather lengthy minute deplored the fact that a Member's wife had been found there with her husband and other male guests. The discretion of the minute writer is such that one cannot determine the fate of that Member!

In the minutes of the General Committee meeting of 26 May 1960 under 'Other Business' it is noted: 'The Manager to be advised to look into the following points: Page Boys; Waiters; Window Boxes; Ashtrays; Cleaning of Curtains; Watering of Whiskey'. In June 1965 it was decided to place a cash register in the Members' Bar, 'any bell on same to be silenced', On 3 May 1966 the General Committee meeting minuted: 'Mitchell and Son Limited: Letter certifying that a sample of gin taken from Club Bar for test (following a verbal query of its quality) was in same condition as supplied by the distillery which made it'. Matters of perhaps more moment were to occupy the 1970s: on 26 April 1973 there is the first mention of a Development Committee under the chairmanship of Dermot O'Reilly-Hyland together with John Meagher, Tom Brindley, Gerry Hickey, Richard Hurley, Bill Lennox and Maurice Tempany. It reported to a special meeting of the General Committee on 17 May. In essence it would appear that

Annual Dinner 1977.
(l to r): Harold Quinlan,
Trustee; His Excellency
President P. J. Hillery;
Brendan Mathews,
Chairman and Michael
Kennedy, Honorary
Secretary, with Mary
Hennessy, the longest-
serving staff member who
celebrates her 24th year
with the Club during the
Sesquicentennial

the proposals (described as a master survey and not a master plan by
one committee member) would have cost about £125,000. By the
end of the meeting the Development Committee had been thanked
for their work and disbanded and a piecemeal job of not more than
£50,000 on Dining Room and kitchen together with painting and
similar maintenance and doing up the staff quarters was agreed.
Additionally the Chairman received a mandate to get the dowdy look
off the Hall, Dining Room and possibly Reading Room as these were
a deterrent to guests.

1976 was the year of the Herrema kidnapping and the death of
Frank Stagg on hunger-strike in Britain. On 19 February the minutes
included the following: 'Front door: a formal request from the Gardai
that due to the current unrest the front door should be kept closed
when the Hall Porter's lodge was not manned, was discussed. It was
agreed to accede to this request and install an extension bell in the
Service Room'. From June to September of the same year all the Irish
banks were on strike. The Club overcame the problem by dealing
with the Bank of America.

John A. Costello, leader of the first coalition government which
took office in 1954, was elected an Honorary Member for the period
of his term as Taoiseach. On 25 November 1976 it was agreed that

the President of Ireland, Dr Patrick Hillery, should be offered Honorary Membership for his term of office. On 16 December it was decided, however, to offer him Honorary Life Membership. He accepted and has subsequently made regular use of the Club.

The writers of minutes of committees of the Club over the period from 1945–1990 have discharged their duties with great circumspection. Despite that fact, however, it is abundantly clear that the success of the Club is very largely due to the commitment and dedication of successive Chairmen and their committees who have managed to keep it in being through difficult times. In the same period both in Dublin and London many similar clubs have gone to the wall through lack of patronage. Certainly on many occasions the Stephen's Green Club minutes show near panic by some committees. A variety of measures, such as closing the upper floors and reletting them, of merging with the Hibernian United Services Club or, more recently, relocation, were given serious consideration. Thankfully none of the committees succumbed to these temptations and Members currently enjoy substantially unchanged facilities.

There is a strange but continuous ethos governing the conduct of Members of the Club which does not exist elsewhere. In this writer's humble opinion its cornerstone is the disapproval of discussion by Members, either amongst themselves or with guests, of matters commercial or professional within Club premises. The obligation of surrendering one's briefcase or papers to the Porter on entry empha- sises the social nature of its activities. These disciplines remove at once the opportunity to exploit contact with fellow Members which exist in other organisations of a similar nature.

The nomination and election of new Members has been a careful exercise which has stood the test of time. A new Member, on election, invariably finds himself cordially welcomed and accepted by his peers. The camaraderie of spirit that has cemented Members both old and young is notable. In the early '50s there appears to have been a predominance of membership from the legal and medical professions but these have been joined in more recent times by an increased representation from what is termed the financial services sector of our community. Other clubs attract a greater proportion of commercial- based membership as they facilitate completion of business trans- actions. The Stephen's Green Club has retained its repute as a safe and calm harbour to which Members can repair from the pressures of their chosen careers and enjoy a high standard of food and wine and the companionship of those of like mind.

The Captains and the Kings

JAMES S. McCARTHY

James S. McCarthy

Monday. Lunchtime. Club table. This is the place to be after any special sporting event – the British Open, Wimbledon, The Horse Show – and rarely is conversation more animated than after Rugby International weekends. The scene is a familiar one, Ireland have just been beaten by England; depression reigns supreme. Everyone a Monday morning quarterback and all assume selectorial duties. The arguments are cogent, the analysis concise. Some issue their verdict with judicial authority: "Heads must roll. The commitment is gone. The skills are not there any more". Others are more melancholy: "Where is the flair, where is the fire, where are the glory days of long ago?" And others are simply disbelieving: "Is the spirit of adventure gone from Irish Rugby? Did I really hear that the coach now tells the players what to eat? What will he tell them next? O'Reilly and Mulligan would have broken his heart".

As the debate progresses and lunch hour lengthens, the present team's inadequacies tend to be compounded when we reflect through rose tinted glasses on those who held their places in days gone by and in that regard we in the Stephen's Green Club are spoilt for choice. Has any other club, of whatever hue, a greater roster of distinguished rugby personalities and as names are proffered and deeds recalled, we tend to favour our own.

Through the years the membership has included many Irish captains: Eugene Davy, Karl Mullen, Tom Grace, Tom Kiernan, Ray McLoughlin and the writer. The number of past presidents include Davy again, Jack Coffey, Paddy Madigan, Tom Kiernan and the late Cahir Davitt. We have had numerous selectors and committee men including some of the above and, of course, the late Tony Brindley. Michael Cuddy was our last chairman of the Irish selectors.

Eugene Davy: what a wonderful player. He was capped 34 times for Ireland in the 'twenties and 'thirties and, I need hardly say, all the caps were the same size. Was he better than Jack Kyle? We will never know. Eugene says he was not and of course Jack says he must have been, but what else would you expect either Eugene or Jack to say? E. O'D Davy holds the unique distinction of scoring three tries for Ireland against Scotland at Murrayfield in 1930 in the first half. Typical of Eugene, however, he decided he was overdoing things and played it cool in the second half. He also played on an Irish team where his club, Lansdowne, supplied all of the three-quarter line: Arigho, Crowe, Davy and Lightfoot. He scored eight tries and two dropped goals for Ireland in his illustrious career.

Another member, Ham Lambert, also of Lansdowne was a great all-round sportsman, playing rugby and cricket for Ireland and becoming an international referee when he retired from playing the game.

The late Paul Murray, an outstanding footballer who played for Wanderers, was capped for Ireland in three different positions behind the scrum. He kicked a record of four conversions against Scotland in 1932. The next day the *Sunday Independent* carried the headline: 'Murray's Day at Murrayfield'.

Bethel Solomons (*painting by Estella Solomons*).

Karl Mullen of Old Belevdere, a great and most successful captain, led Ireland to two Triple Crown victories and skippered our only Grand Slam team in 1948. He also captained the Lions' 1950 tour of New Zealand and Australia. I can still remember him as he led the Irish team out of the dressing room, turning and saying: "Now, lads, all I'll ask of you today is for God's sake get your retaliation in first". An oft-repeated phrase.

Tony O'Reilly, a man of wit and wisdom, a true Corinthian, broke all the records and all the rules. Always considered that a coach was there for taking the team to the game. Toured South Africa in 1955 when he was just out of school and New Zealand in 1959 where his record number of tries has never been equalled. O'Reilly is only one of three Irishmen who have played for their country in three decades – the 'fifties, the 'sixties and the 'seventies. He has always insisted that playing rugby was for fun and enjoyment, even though winning was also a vital ingredient, hence all those tries. Was there anyone who got more fund out of the game than O'Reilly and his great friend, Mulligan? – they remain an institution. I was with the man himself when he was hauled out of Ronnie Scott's Jazz Club and told he was to play against England at Twickenham the following day even though he considered himself in semi-retirement. He was advised by Willie John McBride that his best plan of defence was to shake his jowls at his opposite number: "It'll frighten the daylights out of him, O'Reilly".

I first met Tony when I was a veteran on the Irish team, one of the elite who actually called the selectors by their first names. I asked

Ronnie Kavanagh, after a team meeting: "Who is the new boy with the red head?" He replied: "That's Tony O'Reilly and I can tell you, Macker, he is here to stay and you'll be hearing a lot about him". Little did I know. The next day we played against France. I can't remember who won or what the score was but I do vividly remember the *Sunday Independent* report on the game stating that McCarthy must now be nearing the end of a distinguished career, as on two occasions he badly missed a tackle on O'Reilly's opposite number Maurice Prat. I've never worked out why the hell he didn't tackle him himself. However, in omitting to mention that O'Reilly and Prat played in the centre and I played in the forwards, the reporter had better commercial foresight than rugby knowledge.

Fergus Slattery, a really great wing forward. How I would have loved to have played for Ireland with him. Slattery played outstanding rugby all over the world for Ireland and the Lions, but never better than in the famous Barbarians v All Blacks game in 1973 when two great teams showed us how rugby can really be played and Slattery showed what a great wing forward he was. Was there really only one Fergus Slattery playing that day for the Barbarians?

Tom Grace played for Ireland from 1972 to 1978 and captained the side in 1976/77, winning 25 caps and scoring some wonderful tries, none better than in 1973 when he scored a last minute try to give Ireland a 10 points all draw which is the best result they have ever achieved against the All Blacks.

Ray McLoughlin, an outstanding captain of Ireland who played in the 'sixties and 'seventies. He also played with distinction for the Lions on two tours in 1966 and 1971. For many years Ray played what he described as "religious rugby": "it is better to give than to receive". For Ray the game was all about blood, toil, tears, sweat and embro-cation. Three o'clock on Saturday started on Wednesday afternoon. What a marvellous coach he would make for Ireland even today, or does distance lend enchantment to the scene?

We have a new Member in the Club, Tom Kiernan, who must have played for Ireland for at least a century. He captained Ireland and the Lions and, of course, was a wonderful full-back. It was he who coached the Munster Rugby team and fired them with the passion that brought victory over the All Blacks in 1978 and subsequently went on to coach the international side. He is a member of one of Ireland's most famous rugby families, the Murphy Kiernan dynasty. The number of caps in the clan at present is, I believe, 173 and now with the current incumbent in the full back position, young Kenny Murphy, there is no sign of that flow of caps coming to an end which is great for the family and better for Ireland. I wonder does it mean that great footballers are born and rarely made.

IRELAND
(GREEN)

REF...
MR. R. A...
(Scottish R...

FULL BACK:
15. G. NORTON .... Bective Rangers

THREEQUARTERS:
14. M. LANE (Right Wing) .... Univ. College, Cork
13. W. D. McKEE (Right Centre) .... N.I.F.C.
12. T. J. GAVIN (Left Centre) .... London-Irish
11. B. O'HANLON (Left Wing) .... Dolphin

HALF BACKS:
10. J. W. KYLE (Stand Off) .... Queen's University
9. E. STRATHDEE (Scrum) .... Queen's University

FORWARDS:
1. A. A. McCONNELL .... Collegians
2. K. MULLEN (Capt.) .... Old Belvedere
3. T. CLIFFORD .... Young Munster
4. C. CALLAN .... Lansdowne
5. J. E. NELSON .... Malone
6. J. W. McKAY .... Queen's University
7. D. J. O'BRIEN .... London-Irish & Old Belvedere
8. J. McCARTHY .... Dolphin

Touch Judge: MR. E. J. DOYLE (I.R.F.U.)

Ball presented by Messrs. Gilbert's through their...

FIRST AID SERVICE BY THE ST. JOHN AMBULANCE BRIGADE OF IRELAND

PROGRAMME
WITH CORRECT N... R PLAYERS
IR... RBY... L UNION

IRELAND
v.
ENGLAND

LANSDOWNE ROAD
SATURDAY,
FEBRUARY 12th, 1949.
KICK-OFF 3 p.m.

3D

ELVERY'S
ARE **GOOD**
FOR *Rugger* SUPPLIES

We can speak of others, many of whom sat for lunch or dinner in this famous Dining Room: many great and distinguished club players who of course are the backbone of the game in Ireland. Other Members are recalled: Terence Millen for instance, Trinity College Captain and Ireland's only lst five eight. H.M. Reid, a Country member for many years. Formed a brilliant half back combination with the famous Dicky Lloyd. They played together for Trinity College and Ireland from 1910 to 1913. Dr Bethel Solomons played for Trinity and Ireland before the First World War, 1908 to 1910.

And so the talk rambles on, the Club table usually a haven of serenity amidst the hustle and bustle of a busy city, and perhaps time for one last topic. What are our chances in the World Cup? "None", replies a senior member, "unless we want to be as single-minded and committed as they are in the Southern Hemisphere". "My Goodness", comments someone else, "Did you hear about the advertisement in the *Christchurch Star*:

> REFINED GENTLEMAN wishes to meet cultured widow.
> View matrimony.
> Must have independent means
> and 2 tickets to the 3rd test.
> Please send photograph. Of tickets.

Enough. Monday. Lunchtime over. Two hours, Good fun, great company, great club.

Ireland won 14-5 on the way to their second successive Triple Crown. Captain, Karl Mullen, No.8, J. S. McCarthy

137

In re ludi cum fustibus

MICHAEL G. O'CONNOR

Michael G. O'Connor

The history of golf in relation to The Stephen's Green Club is not dissimilar to that of golf in Ireland as a whole. Generally speaking golf achieved some popularity after 1900 and many of the clubs which are well established today were founded between that year and 1910. Portmarnock and Royal Dublin are exceptions since golf was played on those seaside links before the turn of the century.

The most significant record of golfing interest associated with the Club is the fact that two cups – the Stephen's Green Cup and the Autumn Cup – were presented in 1912, the latter a trophy for veterans. The initial name inscribed on the Stephen's Green Cup is that of D. Lister in 1912. The second name to appear is Louis Meldon in 1914, who belonged to a family more associated with cricket than golf. The first name on the Autumn Cup is that of the Convenor, C.O. Martin, the first captain. Membership of the Club included some early enthusiasts for the game such as Frank Fottrell who was born in 1878 and played at Royal Dublin off a handicap of scratch. John Lumsden and his son, Dr. John, were also members – the latter being associated with the founding of the Royal Dublin Club as well as being donor of The Lumsden Cup, a trophy for those in the single figure range of handicap. The Lumsden Cup Competition is run each year at a different club and has achieved much popularity complemented by a very large number of entrants.

The advent of the Great War leaves us with no golfing records until 1920 when there was a short renewal of activity. However, there was very little interest in the game again until after 1945. The 'fifties was also a period of apathy. Nevertheless, from 1967 onwards golf had an upsurge of interest and since then the Cups have been played for each year.

Some very interesting and notable names are inscribed on the trophies in recent times including that of Tommy Brindley – a cousin

Tommy Brindley

of Basil's. Tommy was Chairman of the Leinster Branch and subsequently President of the Golfing Union of Ireland. P.F. Murray is another of the names to appear. Paul was capped at rugby for Ireland and was also no mean golfer, being runner up to R.H. Saunders in the South of Ireland Championship of 1934. He subsequently won 'The South' in 1940 and was captain of Milltown Golf Club in 1942.

Both Michael Fitzpatrick and Bill Thompson have played at Inter-Provincial level and are renowned as competitors of considerable calibre. Michael was, by common consent, adjudged unlucky when beaten in the semi-final of the Close Championship at Malone in 1956. He also had the distinction of being elected President of the Golfing Union of Ireland in 1983. There is, however, one name which appears on both the Stephen's Green Cup and the Autumn Cup which is synonymous with golfing success and outstanding achievement at the highest level – that of J.B. Carr.

Joe, as all golfers well know, has had a meteoric career as an amateur golfer with three victories in the Amateur Open Championship, as well as victories in all of the Irish Championships including the Close, many for a record breaking number of times. Joe was captain of the Walker Cup team twice, and holds the record for most appearances at nine and most consecutive appearances at eight. In addition his two sons Roddy and John have been capped for Ireland, while Roddy set a record by following in his father's footsteps as a Walker Cup player. Joe has still found time to play in some of our Club outings and his presence has

Andrew Horne

always been a stimulus to his less skilful fellow golfers – he has won both of our Cups as well as our admiration.

Peter Townsend is the Club Professional at Portmarnock and is an enthusiastic Member of our Club. He has the distinction of having played on the Walker Cup team before he joined the professional ranks and he was subsequently selected and played on the Ryder Cup team. On a more modest golfing level the records indicate that M.G. O'Connor won the Stephen's Green Cup on three occasions while F.C. Martin, Tommy Brindley, John Bolger, Tony Walsh, Vincent Nolan and David Callaghan captured it twice. The Autumn or Veterans' Cup, on the other hand, has been won four times by Michael Fitzpatrick while Sean Mullan, Cyril Myerscough and Bill Lennox won on two occasions.

In 1957 another cup was presented to the Club by H.W. Murphy and J.J. Hickey, and was engraved as 'The Next Door Cup'. This trophy is for competition between ourselves and our neighbour – the Hibernian United Services Club. Regrettably the records show that it was played for on only five occasions, the last being in 1977. The balance of the matches to date has been in favour of our neighbour by three matches to two. Many members of the older generation will remember J.J. Hickey who was a keen member of the Club and a Director of Brown Thomas & Co.

Professor John Dunne, who joined the Green in 1937, was also a member at one time of 'The Services', and has played for both clubs. John has always been a regular player and enjoys his golf. Some years ago he played a most remarkable stroke. Each winter migrant Brent Geese feed along the estuary which adjoins the course at Portmarnock.

While playing the eleventh hole John's tee shot struck a flying goose and killed it.

Other well known figures who are or were members of the Green and who have shown an interest in golf include Jim McCarthy, former Irish International wing forward and member of one of our Triple Crown winning teams. Jim is a very keen golfer and plays much of his golf at Portmarnock off a handicap of six. Mention must also be made of former member Kevin Troy who was selected to play for Ireland at golf. Deceased members who were well known include Dr. Andrew Horne, W.E. Wylie and Sir Joseph Glynn. Professor Pierce Purcell, a former President of the Golfing Union of Ireland and his son Des Purcell who was an international bridge player must also be mentioned as all wielded a club on occasion.

It has been said that one half of golf is great fun, the other half is putting which is sometimes no fun at all. To roll a ball of circa 1½ inches in diameter into a hole of 4¼ inches in diameter has often created havoc among golfers and on occasion prompted assaults, suicides and even divorces. There is nothing in the world of sport that produces such extremes of emotion as the black art of putting. Despite that, however, most golfers enjoy the healthy benefits derived from this unique and relaxing sport which is usually conducted in a variety of splendid natural settings. Its popularity today gives testimony to that fact.

It is regrettably becoming more and more difficult at the present time to get on a course even when enjoying the membership of a Club. One has to be quick off the mark to get one's name on a time sheet, especially at weekends when most courses are crowded. This aspect is one of the problems which outings have to face and the Green outing is no exception. The position has been aggravated in recent years by the fact that many are taking early retirement and as a consequence more and more golfers seek to play not only at weekends but on weekdays as well. Leisure is likely therefore to be the business opportunity of the twenty-first century.

In recent years the venue for the annual golf outing has been Milltown Golf Club; however, other courses including Sutton and Portmarnock have been played. As indicated previously the upsurge in popularity of golf has made it more and more difficult to procure a venue for our annual outing, more particularly since it is long established practice and indeed tradition for the Members of 'The Green' to return to no. 9 for their Annual Golf Dinner, thereby depriving the venue club of revenue. Our grateful thanks are therefore due to Milltown. The Golf Dinner has been very well supported over recent years and is one of the major sporting occasions of our Club.

The Old Bridge Room

NOEL PEART

Noel Peart

When I joined The Stephen's Green Club in 1947 the Card Room was a very lively area indeed. It was rarely empty and I have seen sessions last until half-past three in the morning. The main game played was unquestionably bridge, although high-stake poker games were not unknown to take place; but the participants were very tight-lipped about them, so I cannot comment.

There was an afternoon session every day of the week lasting from about five until seven or seven thirty. At seven the participants usually drifted away and went home. I usually played on Monday afternoons because there was a big game on Monday night. After the afternoon session I went down to dinner and then went up for the Monday night game.

I do remember affectionately many of the distinguished afternoon players. Some of them have played their last rubber. One of them, who very happily is still a member of the Club, was James Davy. Another was Dr. Atkinson-Stoney, a very distinguished professional whose hearing gradually became more and more defective until he passed out of the game. Then there was Judge Willie Wylie, who had been the Judicial Commissioner of the Land Commission until he retired. My father, who was a Land Commission Solicitor, practically knelt down and kissed the ground at the mention of his name. He considered that all Land Commission Law ended when Judge Wylie retired. Who am I to say he was wrong? I remember Norman Chance, one of four distinguished brothers. He was a great enthusiast. I played with him in the Rubber Bridge Competition one year and we reached the final. We were playing two opponents who, I think, would have to be reckoned superior to us as a partnership. Norman said to me: "What are the tactics, what are the tactics?" I replied, "Down the middle, and let the cards win for us". He was delighted. Rightly so, I think. We played down the middle, and after four rubbers we were

142

4,500 points ahead (which is an untouchable lead) and we all went down to dinner. Poor Norman died the following year, but at least he died the champion.

I recall one other player, although his name escapes me. He had been a major in the British Army and looked every bit of it. His manner was brusque, and his moustache bristling. When he made a claim at the end of a hand, he had the endearing habit of laying down his cards with the announcement, "These are all cock birds". I never heard the expression before or since, but I remember him for it.

When we went up after dinner, the standard of bridge was appreciably higher. A number of the players had played for Ireland and many of those who had not were practically as good. Just like the five o'clock game, I can name one member of the school who is still with us: the apparently immortal Professor John Dunne. I played with him in the first Bridge Tournament that was ever organised in the Stephen's Green Club, and we won it on a most dangerous slam (bid by the Professor, I need hardly say); nobody who knows him will be in any way surprised at this piece of information.

There were several other doctors. Andrew Horne, son of Sir Andrew Horne, was a distinguished gynaecologist. There was Bethel Solomons: I have an idea he played international bridge for Ireland, but I know he played international rugby. He was, in fact, the hero of the immortal story of the tram driver from whom he inquired:

First Contract Bridge International, Ireland v England, 1932.
Teams and officials (l to r): Standing: Ewart Kempson, Mrs McCormack, G. Tierney, J. B. Shortt, Mrs Maxwell Henry, C. Matheson; Seated: Mrs Holmes Wilson, Mrs Lambert, Col. Buller, Mrs Gordon Eivers, Col. Beasley; On ground: Mrs Browne, H. Williams, H. G. Freehill

143

"Who do you think will win the match?" "What match?" said the tram driver. "England v. Ireland," said Bethel, who was going to play in the match. "Ireland", said the tram driver, and spat out of the tram: "Fourteen Protestants and a Jew". But he was a great and kindly man, and a wonderful gynaecologist who had been Master of the Rotunda. And that leaves 'Drew' Davidson, who was also Master of the Rotunda, (although not simultaneously, of course). 'Drew' was a first-class player who could not get it out of his head that he was the unluckiest player in the world. This is not a winning attitude at rubber bridge. Another of our doctors was Frank McMenamin. Frank was a well-known and distinguished international bridge player, somewhat irascible, but with an endearing habit. If anyone sneezed, he always said "God bless you; if it isn't snuff."

We weren't all doctors. There was the very distinguished actor, Paul Farrell. He was, as actors are, up-and-down, but he finished *up*.

Cartoon by Frank Reynolds
(see illustration, p.105).

144

He played the part of the old tramp in *Last Exit to Booklyn* and he must have come home with a tidy sum. My painful memory is that I saw the film and was horrified to see my old friend being kicked to death by the skinheads in the Brooklyn Tunnel. Even on the film it shook me. We had a Swede, too: Svante Lignell, who died of a heart attack in a cabin on the mail boat on his way to England. Svante was a totally unflappable player, and was never known to criticize his partner. The perfect Swede, in other words.

I well remember Seamus Woods, an accountant, advised by his doctors to take up an open-air career. He bought a bag and stood up as a bookmaker. As he had a genius for estimating odds, this was very much to his financial advantage. As it happens, Seamus had also been the Chief-of-Staff of the I.R.A. in Belfast during the Anglo-Irish War, and it was said that there was still a price on his head there. I don't know if there was. He certainly went up, though, whenever he felt like it, which was fairly often, and nobody ever claimed the price. I also remember David Coyle, who had the endearing habit of playing no conventions. It didn't make him the easiest of partners, but he was a good card-player, and everybody managed fairly well. I wouldn't think that David finished a loser on balance. A good player who may have finished a loser (and he was certainly an international) was Pat Lynch. I had known him well when he played international bridge and usually partnered his brother, Inspector John Lynch. They were a formidable pair, but I think Pat was one of the unusual people I have known who really did hold bad cards as a rule. Still, he certainly made the most of them. Perhaps Pat didn't lose after all.

Of my own contemporaries – and school-mates indeed, for we were all in class together in St. Gerard's – were Gerry Read and Desmond Purcell. Gerry both played for Ireland and acted as non-playing captain for many years. The teams who played under him liked him and respected him as a captain because he worked very hard for them. It is important for an Irish team that the captain studies the programme in advance and plans his strategy so that he does not overplay his best players but has them available for the tough matches. He was a pretty exciting partner to play with, however. Desmond Purcell was a very fine player indeed. He played all his international bridge with his brother, Gerry (who also unhappily died young) but I won the Men's Pairs Championship of Ireland with him three times out of three starts, which is not a bad achievement. But Desmond was a marvellous partner. Playing with him, you never expected to get into trouble, and you very rarely did.

We used to play for 50p. a hundred (a very large stake at the time). The largest amount I ever recall winning in a single night was

£122.00. I cannot say that this represented 24400 points because as the night wore on the stakes were invariably increased and by three in the morning it was becoming a big game. Under some weird dispensation of the then Committee, we paid 'fines' on the stroke of each hour after midnight. I think it was to pay overtime to the waiters who kept us regularly supplied with rounds of drink. Nobody would dare to do it now, but there were no breathalysers in those days and I have never heard of anyone having an accident. Of course, playing for those stakes, you needed your wits about you, but to-day, that wouldn't save you from the breathalyser.

That's how it was when I started playing. I wouldn't have missed it for the world.

A Clubbable Man

LORD KILLANIN

Lord Killanin

I have always enjoyed clubs since my undergraduate days, and was the third or fourth generation elected to the County Club in Galway at the age of 19. Looking through my records it would appear that I have been a member of nearly as many clubs as I have held directorships of companies. They include not only three Dublin clubs but two yacht clubs in Dun Laoghaire as well as sporting clubs, whether rugby, or cricket or tennis. My children's generation are not club joiners as was mine; although I gave the advice that if they wished to join a club it should be done early in life – before too much is known about you!

In my first term in Cambridge I was elected to the exclusive Pitt Club but was never able to use it after the first few weeks of term when I was posted on the board for not having paid my bill. Undergraduates had to eat a number of dinners in College but this was a matter of marking oneself in and then proceeding to the Pitt for a good dinner, followed by vintage port and cigars – the finest Havanas at 9d and the best Cockburn at 5s a bottle. The Pitt was not kind to all its members. There was one boring small American who used to sit reading *The Times*. Members sometimes put a match to his paper and he would stay in the chair holding it until the flames reached the fingers of his outstretched arms.

The Cambridge University Footlights Club, which only had a snack luncheon of sardines and cheese, was my favourite. I was elected president in my second year and this, together with my experience of editing a university newspaper, enabled me to obtain my first job in Fleet Street. I do not think I was ever asked about my academic qualifications until I was awarded honorary degrees when I had to confess that although I had the letters MA after my name, the degree, as at Trinity College, Dublin, was purchasable after three years and that obtaining the initial BA was not difficult then. I have had to

admit to my sponsors that my academic life was not distinguished –
but then many of my contemporaries did not even obtain the bad
degree that I did!

My grandfather, when Lord Chief Justice of Ireland, was ineligible
for the Kildare Street Club because he was not 'landed gentry'. Being
a Catholic Trinity graduate he was eligible for the University Club
which, until some years after the second war, was restricted to Trinity
and Oxbridge graduates, although a small number of vacancies were
allowed to others: one, I recall, was Jack B. Yeats. My uncle and pre-
decessor, who was possibly more a landlord and Castle Catholic, was a
member of the Kildare Street and a very good friend and associate of
Edward Martyn, his neighbour in Galway, who was the only Nationalist
Catholic member at that time and taunted the Protestant Ascendancy
by saying the Rosary in the large bay window overlooking Nassau
Street. I followed in my uncle's footsteps and was elected a member of
the Kildare Street Club before the war; but it had always been my
ambition to be a member of the Stephen's Green. It had a liberal
approach to all matters, which is understandable given its history. On
leave during the war I was in what I believed to be the Stephen's
Green Club and said I would like to be a member. I received an
intimation in Normandy that I had been elected. . . to another club
in St. Stephen's Green. I had had such a good evening that I had
mistaken the club I was in, but was subsequently elected to the
Stephen's Green Club in 1950.

I was not much at home in the Kildare Street Club after the war.
When I stayed there while living in Galway I used to hear some
members talking about the "terrible government". It was some time
before I realised they were discussing Westminster and not Leinster
House: there was an influx of English members in the 'flight from
Moscow'. The Kildare Street Club is no longer the entity it was. The
Stephen's Green Club has maintained its independence – at a financial
cost but not at the cost of lowering the standard either of membership
or of facilities or amalgamation.

Before the war I was elected a member of the Garrick in London,
having been proposed and seconded by Gerald Duckworth, the publisher, and the then Master of the Rolls. I was employed as a reporter
on the *Daily Mail*. The first day after election I did not hesitate to go
to the Club where the members sit at the one large table. Much the
youngest present, I was asked my profession. I replied that I was a
reporter on the *Daily Mail*. That cleared the table, and the next time I
went in my proposer said: "Michael, I think in future when you are
asked it would be better to say you are a Peer of the Realm". In January
1990, having read of the case of the litigious editors I realised that the

Garrick today has many journalists, but in 1937 they were confined to dramatic critics. One important element in club life is that officially no business is transacted, although unofficially many members now have their subscriptions paid. After the war in the Garrick I asked, with trepidation, for a receipt for a single lunch as I had to account for my expenses in London. There was no hesitation, for "Sure all the members now ask for receipts for their accounts". If briefcases and the papers

Lord Morris, the author's grandfather *('Spy' cartoon, 'Vanity Fair').*

are forbidden, in my experience as a company director the placing of key employees in clubs is done for strategic reasons. This has not been a bad thing as it has enabled clubs to survive and elect suitable members; but if overdone and money were to dictate it would be like international sport, which is no longer sport for fun but sport for money.

When I took my seat in the House of Lords in 1935, not knowing the protocol I sat by chance on the Conservative/Unionist benches. As a result I was approached by a peer who told me I should join the Carlton Club – which I did. After one dinner there I realised I was neither a Conservative nor a Unionist. It was an expensive dinner as I had paid the entrance fee and one year's subscription besides the meal.

I lived at one time in the R.A.C. in Pall Mall where I swam each day. Bernard Shaw would walk across St. James's Park to swim also and I recall that his beard went out in front of him as if it were floating on a frame on the water instead of trailing behind his head. I had to resign from the R.A.C. for the same reason that I was posted in the Pitt Club in Cambridge. I was also elected to the exclusive Beefsteak Club which, like the Garrick, was now male and member-orientated. There was little encouragement to bring visitors. Ladies are still not permitted there although they are now allowed as guests at the Garrick every day.

In my club life I have avoided being on committees, except of the Footlights: this is not a very clubbable quality, especially when one is apt to be a hurler on the ditch. An exception was the Irish Club in London, as I was instrumental in its foundation and the first president. The Club arose from an amalgam of people from the London Irish Rugby Club, the old Four Provinces Club and the Shamrock Club, which had been founded for Irishmen serving in the British forces during the war. An early meeting in my mother's flat was attended by, amongst others, the poet Denis Devlin, then at the embassy, and Cyril Cusack. The intention was to have a club for white-collared Irish workers who would not be eligible for the London West End clubs nor wish to be engulfed in ceili halls in Kilburn or Hammersmith. My main contribution was to insist they obtained the best possible premises – hence the Club's arrival at 82 Eaton Square. There were tempting offers from Notting Hill, Bayswater and other areas. After some years as president I could no longer devote the time needed as the Club increased in strength – and in internal frictions. In due course I even ceased to be a vice-president although my wife – who opened the club – and myself are life members.

A unique article in the lease from the Westminster estate related to the keeping of animals on the premises. I presumed this to refer to dogs and cats. Some thought this was an insult to Ireland, and I went

Philip Love, enjoyed
the good fellowship at
the Club as well as his
bloodstock, rugby and
golf: the quintessentially
'clubbable man'.

to see the late Duke of Westminster, then living near Lismore, and as a result the offending clause was removed. I assume that 82 is the only house in Eaton Square where animals are not forbidden. Another feature of the Irish Club's lease was its previous identity as Orange House, as Queen Wilhelmena of the Netherlands had made it her home during the war. It certainly began, and I am sure remains, apolitical, with all shades of membership – green and orange.

Alas, I do not now use the Stephen's Green Club as much as I would like to, but I feel indebted to be asked to contribute to this important anniversary which coincides with the bicentenary of the Turf Club, of which I am also a member and former steward. I am still very happy to be able to 'totter' in and meet my many friends, and I trust that it will remain in years to come in its historic and magnificent Dublin house, which is part of our heritage. My sincere hope is that it will survive and thrive along with its convivial and friendly membership. Clubs are primarily for friendship – but also for eating and drinking at reasonable prices. Most have had to increase membership fees to meet overheads, but this has not necessarily meant that the calibre of members has declined – certainly not in the case of the Stephen's Green. I recall that in one club, however, which always had a crowd of loafers standing outside, a member returning after the war asked the snobbish head waiter what the club was like nowadays. The reply was: "Well, sir, them that used to be outside does now be inside".

BIOGRAPHIES I
1840 – 1875

It has been said that all history is just biographies. Yet they can make turgid reading. A litany of dull folk – then a few meagre facts about some intriguing personality.

BERNAL (OSBORNE), RALPH. 1808–82. Capt., 7th Royal Fusiliers, was an Extra Aide de Camp in the household of the Viceroy, Mulgrave, until elected to parliament in 1841 in the Liberal interest. A witty and sympathetic speaker on Irish topics at Westminster until he retired in 1874. Married 1844 Catherine, only daughter of Sir Thomas Osborne of Newton Anner, Clonmel, Co. Tipperary and took the name Bernal-Osborne. Bernal came of a wealthy Jewish family in London after the style of his more successful Conservative rival Benjamin Disraeli. He would have had sympathy with O'Connell's defence of the legal rights of the Jews. Served on the foundation committee of the Union Club, February 1837, probably at the request of Mulgrave. Also a member of the Reform Club, London. (See also ROSENTHAL).

BERWICK, WALTER QC. Called to the Bar 1826 and resided at 9 Lr. Fitz-william St. with Edward and John Berwick. Assistant Barrister for Waterford and held in esteem by O'Connell. A petitioner for the Letters Patent. Union Club committee February 1839 and went on to serve as Trustee of the SGC. Berwick became a Judge of Her Majesty's Court of Bankruptcy and Insolvency. His probate showed 'effects under £1,800'. Charles James Trench (q.v.) was an executor.

BLAKE, ANTHONY RICHARD MP. 1786–1849. Youngest son of Martin Blake MP of Ballyglunin and Hollypark, Co. Galway. Educ. Clongowes 1828–33. Although a Catholic was a member of the administration of Marquess Wallesley; described by a contemporary as 'the backstairs Viceroy of Ireland'. Author of *Thoughts upon the Catholic Question*, 1828. Served on SGC committee 1840/41.

BLAKE, CHARLES JOSEPH JP, BL. Of Heath House, Maryborough (Portlaoise), Queen's Co. (Laois), Trustee of the SGC 1907. Second son of Valentine O'Connor Blake of Towerhill, Co. Mayo. Apparently no direct relation of Anthony Richard Blake.

BRADY, SIR MAZIÈRE. 1876–1871. An original member of the SGC, a Liberal and supporter of the principles of the Queen's University and the arts. Solicitor General for Ireland 1837; Chief Baron of the Court of the Exchequer 1840 (succeeded by D.R. Pigot); Irish Court of Chancery 1846; Baronet (by Gladstone) 1869. Died at Upr. Pembroke St. and succeeded by his son, His Honour Sir Francis W. Brady QC, who presented his portrait to

Sir Mazière Brady

the Club. The Mazière ancestors are buried in the Huguenot cemetery on Merrion Row. (See also PIGOT).

CARNWORTH, Thomas-Henry Dalzell of Clydesdale, Scotland, Earl of Carnworth, married Mary-Anne, daughter of Henry Grattan. Elected to the committee in 1841.

CHAPMAN, SIR MONTAGU-LOWTHER, MP. 1808–1852. Of Killua Castle, Co. Westmeath, came of an old Anglo-Irish family prominent in the House of Commons and the Royal St George Yacht Club (1845). Elected to the SGC committee in 1841/2. T.E. Lawrence ('of Arabia') was the illegitimate son of Sir Montague's nephew Thomas Chapman of South Hill, Delvin, Co. Westmeath.

CLARKE, THOMAS. No biographical trace. Served on the SGC committee from 1840 onwards.

CLONCURRY. 1770–1853. Valentine Browne Lawless, Second Baron Cloncurry of Maretimo, Blackrock and Lyons Castle, Co. Kildare. Served on the first committees and must have been lively company at the Club. His brother Nicholas, 1733–99, made a fortune as a woollen draper and married a Dublin brewery heiress. Both joined the Established Church. Valentine was imprisoned without trial in the Tower of London for two years: understandably this left him with a sour outlook on HM Government. He was a supporter of Daniel O'Connell. In 1833 Cloncurry struck a hard bargain with Vignoles of the Dublin & Kingstown Railway Company. The resultant granite pavilions beside the Leper's Stream still delight observant travellers on the DART. His eldest son, Hon. Edward Lawless, succeeded him as third Baron and was elected to the Union Club committees in 1837 and 1838. Royal St George Yacht Club 1845.

William Cogan

COGAN, WILLIAM HENRY FORD. 1823–94. Barrister, MP 1852–80. An active committee man during his long and important membership 1848–94. The only son of a Dublin merchant, he married Gertrude Ryan in 1858, apparently without issue. A bust was presented to the Club by Dr More Madden in 1900 but has been lost.

CONNELLAN, JAMES CORRY AM. Barrister of 10 Lr. Merrion St., Secretary to the Lord Chancellor and Gentleman-at-Large to the Lord Lieutenant's household. Union Club committee 1837/8.

CORBALLIS, JOHN RICHARD. Barrister, 15 Lr. Baggot St. Served on committees of the Union Club and SGC 1837–40. Was also a member of the Royal St. George Yacht Club.

CURRAN, WILLIAM HENRY. Barrister, of 9 Fitzwilliam Place and Dundrum, youngest son of John Philpot Curran, 1750–1817, who defended the United Irishmen and became Master of the Rolls. Served on the SGC committee from May 1840.

DE BALLINCOURT see ROSENTHAL

DICKSON, SAMUEL. No biographical trace. Served on the committees of the Union Club and the SGC 1839/40.

DRUMMOND, THOMAS R.E. 1797–1840. Born at Edinburgh, he arrived with Mulgrave and Morpeth as Under-Secretary for Ireland, one of the few admirable administrators sent by the British. Died in Dublin, worn out after five years of struggling for just and efficient government. His statue by Hogan is in the City Hall. Drummond's famous blunt aphorism still rings loud and clear after all those intervening years of strife: 'Property has its responsibilities as well as its rights'.

DUNNE, JERMIAH. Wholesale woollen and Manchester merchant, 4 Ussher's Quay. Director of Hibernian Joint Stock Banking Co. Served on committees of the Union Club and SGC 1839/40.

EBRINGTON, VISCOUNT. Hugh, second Earl Fortescue MP. 1783–1861. Succeeded Mulgrave as Lord Lieutenant 1839–41 and continued to support Drummond and the policy of striving for efficient administration, for which he was bitterly attacked in *The Mail*. Served on the first committee of the Reform Club 1836 and would have enjoyed issuing the Letters Patent to the SGC.

FITZ-SIMON, CHRISTOPHER MP. Barrister and landowner of Glencullen, and Golden Ball, Co. Wicklow, clerk of the Crown and Hanaper in the Court of Chancery. Married Daniel O'Connell's daughter Ellen. His brother Nicholas MP ('Fat Simon') was a supporter of O'Connell's Repeal Association. In his official capacity was responsible for affixing the Great Seal to our Letters Patent – and collecting the appropriate fee.

FITZGERALD, PETER N. No biographical information. May have been related to Thomas Fitzgerald MP, Catholic landowner and West India proprietor. Served on the SGC 'Foundation' committee for 1840 only.

FITZPATRICK, J. WILSON MP. Of Rathkeale, was Liberal MP for Queen's County (Laois) in 1837–41 and 1847–52. Served on Union Club Committee for only one year, 1837. Not to be confused with Patrick Vincent Fitzpatrick who organised O'Connell's fund-raising during the Repeal Movement.

GREHAN, GEORGE. Connected by marriage with Patrick Seagrave. Served on the first SGC committee 1840 onwards.

HARMAN. (LATER KING-HARMAN). Of Newcastle, Ballymahon, Co. Longford, an Anglo-Irish family who received immense grants of land in the Cromwellian era. Captain Wentworth Harman, 1610–1714, of the Battle Axe Guards, married (secondly) Frances Shepherd, heiress of Newcastle and had issue (inter alia): Wentworth Harman II, c1682–1758, of Co. Carlow who inherited when his father died. If 9 St Stephen's Green was built in c1730 was it for this Wentworth II that is was built? His son, Wesley, died without surviving issue 1758 leaving the estates to his uncle Robert, 1699–1765 who died without issue.

HARMAN, ROBERT was succeeded by his brother, REV. DEAN CUTTS HARMAN, 1706–65, who was succeeded by his sister Anne's son LAURENCE PARSONS (q.v.), 1749–1807, first Earl of Rosse. The Rev. Cutts Harman became Church of Ireland Dean of Waterford 1759 and died without issue. He presented the organ to Waterford Cathedral but resided at 9 (then 10) St Stephen's Green. As our worthy Dean gazed out from his library window, no doubt he pondered the fate of another Bishop of Waterford who, a century previously was executed on St Stephen's Green for bestiality with a cow. See PETER LA TOUCHE.

HOLBROOKE, HENRY. 'Engraver, lithographer & die-sinker to the Queen for Ireland' at 4 Crow Street, he resided at 14 (now 13) St Stephen's Green. The house was shared with Mathew Moran, glove merchant. Holbrook produced the fine scroll work on the Letters Patent, 1840.

HOWLEY, SIR JOHN QC. 1789–1866. Of 32 Upper Fitzwilliam St., called to the Bar in 1815. Married Sara Roche 1826. Well liked by O'Connell. The Howleys were a wealthy family of merchants and landowners from Rich Hill, Co. Limerick, Knighted 1865. Served on the Union Club committee 1837–39 but did not continue on to the SGC committee.

HUDSON. This family was a most interesting ingredient in the formation of the Club. They were Unionist but refreshingly liberal and ecumenical in outlook. The father Edward, MD, 1742–1821, was born in Cork and became State Dentist at a time when such specialisation was rare. He supported O'Connell's Emancipation and Reform movements. His residence at Rathfarnham (afterwards Pearse's St Enda's school) was an active centre in the early days of Irish Revival letters and music, a tradition continued by his family. Three of his sons were actively connected with the SGC: Edward G., Dean; Henry, State Dentist; William Elliot, lawyer.

HUDSON, REV. EDWARD GUSTAVUS, 1792–1851, was Dean of Armagh (in absentia), preferring to live at 39 Upper Fitzwilliam Street and Glenville, Co. Cork. Almost all of the other Church of Ireland clergymen were strongly opposed to the O'Connell/ Gladstone policies for disestablishment, wider electoral franchise and any weakening of the powers of the Tory landlords.

He was elected to the Union Club committee in 1838/9 and continued as Trustee of the SGC from 1840. As such he was a Grantee of the Letters Patent. Buried at Ardnageely, Co. Cork. HENRY, MD, 1800–1860, of 24 St Stephen's Green, was appointed State Dentist in succession to his father Edward. He served on the SGC committee from 1840. WILLIAM ELLIOTT, 1796–1853, lawyer and scholar, of 39 Fitzwilliam St. Upper, was Taxing Master and a most generous helper in the early movements to preserve Irish literature and music, assisting O'Donovan, O'Daly and James Duffy. Served on the SGC committee from 1840.

LA TOUCHE, PETER. 1733–1828. Successful Huguenot merchant banker who resided at 15 St Stephen's Green, Bellevue, Delgany and Lugalla, Co. Wicklow. After the death of Parsons, Earl of Rosse in 1812, No.9. (then 10) passed into his hands, presumably as a result of a financing transaction. Peter was very charitable—like his father David II of whom it is said that he walked abroad, his pockets full of shillings for the poor. If reproached for indiscriminate giving he would reply: "Si mon shilling tombe à propos une fois sur dix c'est assez". On the other hand the La Touches were bigoted opponents of Catholic Emancipation. Four of the family were members of the Irish parliament which voted against the Union in 1800 – no doubt they could foresee the disastrous fall in property values which did not recover until after the Famine. With his two brothers David and John, Peter was a founding director of the Bank of Ireland in 1783. the family were promoters of the Kildare Street Club in 1782 and served as its Treasurers. Peter La Touche died without issue. Indeed it is strange that the name, so strong a century ago, has now completely died out.

Peter La Touche

LA TOUCHE, ROBERT. Banker, retired Colonel, MP. of Harristown, Co. Kildare. son of John and nephew of Peter. Appears in the Directory as the occupier of no.9 (now no.10) in 1834–6.

LAWLESS, see CLONCURRY.

LEESON, JOSEPH. 1799–1866. Fourth Earl of Milltown, came of a family who made great fortunes first as brewers and then as Georgian property developers. They lived in fine style at Russborough near Blessington, Co. Wicklow. Milltown was the ground landlord of 9 St Stephen's Green.

LYNE, CORNELIUS. 1775–1841. Barrister, of 15 Hume St., was a cousin of Daniel O'Connell and friend of John Philpot Curran. son of Timothy Lyne, merchant, of Cork. He was nicknamed 'Con of the Hundred Bottles' but seems to have been less alcoholic than this suggests. Union Club committee 1837–9; SGC committee 1840.

McCARTHY, ALEXANDER. Educ. Clongowes 1816–22. Barrister of Killorglin Co. Kerry and Dublin. Cousin of Daniel O'Connell. Union Club committee February 1838. Continued on to serve SGC.

McDONALD, NORMAN H. Private Secretary to Morpeth, Chief Secretary for

Ireland. Succeeded Drummond (q.v.) as Under Secretary 1840. SGC committee 1841 for one year.

MAHONY, PIERCE. 1792–1853. MRIA, of Priory House, Stillorgan and Kilmorna, Co. Kerry, was an original member. His bust has a place of honour on the stairs. He was a typically liberal Protestant, an exceptionally successful attorney and O'Connell's family lawyer and confidant in latter years. Mahony was the Parliamentary Agent of the Catholic Association in the last year before the passing of the Emancipation Act in 1829. His two sons Pierce and David carried on practice as solicitors at 43 Dame Street. The family had an embarassing time in 1907 when the 'Irish Crown Jewels' were stolen from the custody of Sir Arthur Vicars, Ulster King of Arms and uncle of Pierce Gun Mahony, Cork Herald. Edward VII was not amused.

MILLTOWN, see LEESON.

MORPETH, VISCOUNT. 1797–1863 George William Howard, seventh Earl of Carlisle, Chief Secretary for Ireland for six years during the Lord-Lieutenancies of Mulgrave and Elrington and at the formation of the Union and SG Clubs. A popular Lord Lieutenant in his own right 1855–58. A fluent, able, kind-hearted gentleman, his statue by Foley is in the Phoenix Park. Formally opened the National Gallery 1862. See PIGOT and BRADY.

Constantine Henry Phipps

MULGRAVE. (1797–1863). Constantine Henry Phipps, MP, second Earl of Mulgrave, elected to parliament as a reforming Liberal and served as Lord Lieutenant of Ireland 1835–9. His presence in the country with Thomas Drummond was full of encouragement for O'Connell and his followers. No doubt Mulgrave would have been most sympathetic with the Union/SGC objectives of justice for Ireland and the reform of the administration system. He was one of the first Trustees of the Reform Club in 1836. His wife and Lady Morpeth were well liked by the young Queen Victoria but were anathema to Robert Peel. In spite of a somewhat frivolous manner Mulgrave was a politician of considerable presence who let some much-needed fresh air into the system of governing Ireland which was as inefficient as it was bigoted.

MULLINS, MICHAEL BERNARD. 1808–1871 JP, CE. Credited with the adaptation of no. 9 after 1840 (See p. 32). Director of the Great Southern Railway and member of the Royal Irish Yacht Club. The obituary in the *Freeman's Journal* was fulsome: 'Very aimable disposition, with high intellectual acquirements . . . contributed largely and without ostentation to . . . charity. He resided a good deal at his country seat at Ballyeagan in King's County [Laois] in which he filled the office of High Sheriff and was held in much esteem by all classes. . .'. The *Irish Builder* noted that he left £30,000 to endow the 'Mullins Convalescent Home'. This was put to good use in the building of the Linden Convalescent Home for the Poor which had been acquired by the Irish Sisters of Charity. Mullins left his library, plus £1200, to his beloved Institution of Civil Engineers where his portrait is preserved. This interesting public figure awaits a biographer.

MULLINS, THOMAS. Barrister, of 39 Lr. Fitzwilliam St., elected to the Union Club committee 1836. May have been a relative of Thomas Mullins, first

Michael Bernard Mullins

Baron Ventry who was associated with O'Connell. Does not seem to have been related to Michael Bernard Mullins, CE, architect to the SGC.

NANGLE, JOHN HYACINTH. 1790–1865. Of Garisker estate, Co. Kildare, he was the last male of a family who came over with Strongbow in 1169. His grandfather and family were spectacularly murdered in 1757 but his father, Christopher, survived. John was educated at Stoneyhurst because the Penal Laws were relaxed in England. He actively supported Catholic Emancipation in 1829. High Sheriff of Kildare 1836, he left no children and the estate passed to his sister Mary. Despite the unusual surname he was no relation of the evangelical clergyman Edward Nangle who organised the Protestant Missionary colony in Achill in 1831.

James O'Brien

NUGENT, SIR PERCY. 1797–1874. Of Donore, Co. Westmeath and Liberal MP for that county. Elected to the Union Club committee in February 1839 and continued on the SGC committees. Son of Commander Thomas Fitzgerald RN, Sir Percy assumed by royal Licence the surname and arms of Nugent. Sarcastic Dubliners dubbed him 'Sir New-Gent'. Married in 1823 a daughter of Walter Sweetman. Despite being Catholic this active family somehow escaped the worst of the Penal Laws. His portrait hangs in the dining room opposite that of his father-in-law. He is shown as a commanding Victorian figure with a walking stick.

O'BRIEN, JAMES. 1806–82. Judge, an original member of the SGC. Born Granard, Co. Longford, a Catholic Liberal MP and Justice of the Queen's Bench. Married Margaret, daughter of Thomas Seagrave and died at his residence on St Stephen's Green.

O'BRIEN, SAMUEL M. Solicitor, of 14 Holles St., was Secretary of the SGC, elected May 1840. Since a Club 'Superintendent', Thomas Atkins, was also appointed, O'Brien was the first of a long line of invaluable Honorary Secretaries. (there is no information about Michael Byrne, secretary of the Union Club 1837–39).

O'CONNELL, DANIEL. See p.42

O'CONNELL, MORGAN. See p. 44

O'CONOR DON, The, of Clonalis and Belangar. This well-known aristocratic family claims descent from the last High King of Ireland. It represents a surprisingly numerous and influential class—the Catholic gentry. The O'Connells, whom they supported as Repealers, came of the same resilient and adaptable historic landlord class who managed to survive the Penal Laws.

O'CONOR, CHARLES OWEN. 1836–1906. DL, LL.B. Succeeded his father Denis in representing Roscommon as Home Rule MP, 1860–80. In 1875 the family owned 12,400 acres in Roscommon with a net annual value of £5,900– a great fortune in those days. A Trustee of the SGC until his death after 37 years of membership.

O'CONOR, DENIS. 1792–1847. Succeeded his father Owen as Liberal MP for Co. Roscommon. A member of the founding committee of the Reform Club, London, in 1836. Presumably was an SGC member but did not serve on the committee.

O'FERRALL, JAMES. Attorney, 17 Lr. Baggot St. The O'Ferrall clan supported O'Connell. Presumably a relative of Redmond More O'Ferrall, 1797–1880, MP, an important Liberal minister. Served on the SGC 'Foundation' committee 1840 for one year only.

Michael O'Loghlin

O'LOGHLIN, SIR MICHAEL. 1789–1842. Of 20 Merrion Square, was O'Connell's favourite junior and the first Catholic judge in Ireland since 1688. As Master of the Rolls was favourably disposed towards the Letters Patent of 1840.

O'MEARA, BARRY EDWARD. 1786–1836. Born in Ireland. Joined British army as assistant surgeon 1804. Obliged to leave 1808 for having assisted at a duel, but secured an appointment in the navy. Serving in HMS *Bellerophon* when Napoleon surrendered himself on board July 1815. Accompanied the ex-emperor to St Helena as his personal physician. Published 1822 *Napoleon in Exile: or a voice from St. Helena.* Died London of erysipelas said to have been caused by catching cold at one of O'Connell's meetings. Founder member of Reform Club, London. His instruments used in treating his imperial patient may be seen in the library of the Royal Academy of Medicine in Ireland, 6 Kildare St.

OSBORNE, see BERNAL.

PARSONS, LAURENCE. 1749–1807. first Earl of Rosse, resided at Newcastle, Co. Longford. He acquired 9 St Stephen's Green through his mother, Anne, a sister of Dean Harman (q.v.). The property then passed to Peter La Touche (q.v.) of Bellevue in 1812. His grand-uncle Laurence, confusingly enough, was also the 'First Earl'. He died 1741 having been a founder member of the satanic Hell Fire Club 1735. This world-famous Birr family also produced two astronomers, a marine engineer and inventor of the turbine and a connection with British royalty through Ann Armstrong-Jones.

The Earl of Rosse: seat and arms

PIGOT, DAVID RICHARD. 1797–1873. An original member of the SGC, son of Dr John Pigot of Kilworth, Co. Cork. Liberal MP 1839–1846, supported O'Connell until the Repeal Movement. Chief Baron of the Exchequer in succession to Sir Mazière Brady 1846–73 (q.v.), the first Catholic to hold this office. Was recognised for a profound knowledge of the law and for con-scientious hearing of evidence. In later years these protracted cases caused complaints—but not from barristers! Also a patron of the arts, particularly of Irish music. With his son John and Mazière Brady were prime movers in founding the National Gallery, 1854. JOHN EDWARD QC, his eldest son, was on the Council of the Young Irelanders 1847–9 and defended William Smith O'Brien and John Mitchel. He then abruptly quit nationalist politics and subsequently made a fortune at the Indian Bar before returning in 1871 to die at the Baron's residence, 15 Merrion Sq. DAVID, the second son, con-tinued the family tradition of high legal achievement which continues to this day in the Club.

PLUNKET. These legal gentlemen are presumed sons of the Lord Chancellor William Conyingham Baron Plunket of 18 St Stephen's Green and Old Connaught, Bray, Co. Wicklow: Hon. PATRICK, barrister, Union Club com-mittee 1837; Hon. DAVID, barrister, Union Club committee 1838; JAMES, QC, SGC committee 1842, etc.

RAPHAEL, ALEXANDER 1775–1850 Was a Christianised London City Jew. He was supported by Daniel O'Connell as member of Parliament for Carlow in 1835 but this was not a happy experience.

ROE, GEORGE MD. 1784–1858. Born Ballyconnell, Co. Cavan where his father Edward was rector. For 42 years surgeon to the Co. Cavan infirmary. His only published paper dealt with an unsuccessful case: 'Fatal effects of chloroform'. Despite this had a lucrative practice from which he amassed a considerable fortune. Friendly with the famous surgeon Sir Philip Crampton and with O'Connell. Elected to the Union Club committee 1838 and served on the SGC committee 1841. Was also an HUSC member.

RORKE, LAURENCE. Barrister, 70 Blessington St. Served on committees of the Union Club and SGC 1839.

ROSENTHAL, HENRY. 1798–1873. 'Alien', a Jewish merchant from Hanover, Germany, who settled in Dublin 1828. He dealt in jewellery, etc. at 19 Royal Arcade, College Green and as tobacconist at 23 Nassau St. Mr Justice Rosenthal was his descendant. The name of Rosenthal's partner (?) Henry Barre De Ballicourt, 'Alien', does not feature in the registers and records of the Jews or Huguenots in Ireland. O'Connell was a zealous defender of the rights of the Jews and was instrumental in the passing of the relieving Acts of 1846/1858 which removed most of their legal disabilities. See also BERNAL and Letters Patent

ROSSE, see PARSONS.

SADLEIR, see p. 52.

SAUSSE, MATTHEW R. Barrister, born Carrick on Suir 1805. Union Club founding committee 1837. Re-emerged on the SGC committees 1844 onwards. Became Chief Justice of Bombay.

SCULLY, VINCENT QC. 1810–1871. Politician from Kilfeacle, Co. Tipperary; MP for Cork 1852 and 1859. Wrote and spoke extensively on the land question. Son of Denys. 1773–1830, political writer. This successful middle-class Catholic family invested in landed property. Another son of Denys was murdered by the Whiteboys in the agrarian troubles of the time. Vincent was elected to the Union Club committee in February 1839 and continued on to the SGC committee.

SEAGRAVE, PATRICK JP. Of the well-known family of Cabra, Co. Dublin which included Sir Henry O'Neal Seagrave, racing motorist and world record waterspeed holder. Patrick was elected to the SGC committee in January 1842.

SMITHWICK, EDMOND 1800–76 Brewer, was Mayor of Kilkenny and local mainstay of Daniel O'Connell. An original member, the family tradition continues at the Club.

SWEETMAN, WALTER. 1798–1882. Barrister, son of John Sweetman, 1752-

1826, who was banished from Ireland for his part in the 1798 rebellion. The family had a successful brewery on Aston's Quay and were strong supporters of O'Connell. Resided at 4 Mountjoy Sq. Was a petitioner for the Letters Patent 1840; served on the Union Club committee 1838/9 and continued as Trustee of the SGC. His only daughter, Elizabeth Maria Eleanor, married 1823 Sir Percy Nugent of Donore. Walter Sweetman's portrait by Sir Thomas Jones, PRHA hangs in the Dining Room. He is depicted as a sensitive figure holding a book in contrast to his stick-bearing son-in-law.

SYMES, THOMAS RADCLIFFE. solicitor, 5 Leinster St. Registrar to the RT. Hon. Baron Richards. SGC committee 1842 only.

SYNGE, CHARLES. Soldier. Born Rathmore, King's Co. (Offaly), 1789; entered army 1809. Present at principal battles in Peninsula and distinguished himself at Salamanca, where severely wounded. Retired as colonel. Lived at Mount Callan, Co. Clare. Died Dublin 1854. Elected to Union Club committee 1837/8.

TIGHE, ROBERT JP. Barrister, of 14 Fitzwilliam Square and one of the few committemen of the Union Club who continued on to serve the SGC. He was Chairman of Co. Limerick. The family had estates at Mitchelstown, Co. Westmeath. Royal St George Yacht Club (1845). Anne Tighe married Benjamin Chapman (q.v.).

TRENCH, CHARLES JAMES QC. 1806–1889. County Court judge of Woodlawn, Co. Galway and Dublin. Third, but second surviving son of Francis Trench of Sopwell Hall, Co. Tipperary, brother of Frederic Trench of Woodlawn. Frederic, though married, must have known that he would have no issue, for when he was to be raised to the peerage in 1800 he had himself created Baron Ashtown with remainder to the heirs of his deceased father. So Francis' eldest surviving son succeeded as second Baron and his brothers and sisters obtained a patent of precedence as Baron's children 1840. Thus C.J. became the Hon. Charles J. Trench. Elected to the Union Club committee 1838 and continued on to the SGC Committee for many years.

BIOGRAPHIES II
1875 to recent times

ARNOTT, MAXWELL (1904). See p. 75.

George Ashlin

ASHLIN, GEORGE COPPINGER. 1837–1921. Born Carrigrenane House, Co. Cork. Partner in firm of Ashlin and Coleman, architects, 7 Dawson St., Dublin from 1902. In partnership with Edward Pugin, son of the more famous A.W. Pugin 1860–70 and with him architect for church of SS Peter and Paul, Cork; St Colman's cathedral, Cobh and the Irish National Exhibition of 1882. His individual work includes the O'Connell Memorial Church, Cahirciveen, Co. Kerry and St Anne's Raheny, Co. Dublin (for Lord Ardilaun). Ashlin married a daughter of A.W. Pugin.

ASHWORTH, CHARLES HERBERT. 1862–1901 (1901) Born in Liverpool, he was an architect with the Dublin Artisans' Dwellings Co. whose offices, in William St., Dublin, he himself designed. Was also responsible for major housing schemes and several buildings of importance in the city and elsewhere.

Charles Ashworth

BAILEY, WILLIAM FREDERICK, CB. (1905) Born Castletown Conyers, Co.. Limerick, educ. TCD. One of the Irish Land Commissioners called to the Irish Bar, 1881. Secretary and President (1902) of the Statistical and Social Inquiry Society of Ireland. Travelled extensively.

BARRY, RALPH BRERETON. (1903) Born Limerick, educ. Clongowes and TCD. County Court Judge of Kildare, Carlow, Wicklow and Wexford. Irish Bar 1880; Professor of Law, Queen's College, Cork, 1884. Prof. of Equity and Practice, King's Inns, Dublin, 1895–8.

BECKETT, WILLIAM F. (c1929). See p. 84.

BEDDY, DR JAMES P. 1901–1976 (1953). An Inspector of Taxes who became Managing Director of the Industrial Credit Corporation during its pioneering years as a merchant bank. Provided economic discourse with Roy Geary and James Meenan (q.v).

Ralph Barry

BEWLEY, CHARLES (1928). Brilliant member of the distinguished Quaker family. Served as Irish Minister to Germany from 1933 until he resigned in 1939. Like many of his contemporaries was more fearful of the spread of communism than of Hitler.

BODKIN, THOMAS. 1887–1961 (1949). Born Dublin, educ. Belvedere, Clongowes and RUI. Called to the Bar and practised until 1916. Dir. of the

National Gallery 1927–35, then first dir. of Barber Institute, Birmingham. Took leading part in negotiations over Hugh Lane collection and his report on the arts (1951) led to the establishment of An Comhairle Ealaíon (Arts Council).

Thomas Bodkin

BOLAND, FREDERICK 1904–1985 (1951). Born Dublin, educ. Merchant Taylors', Clongowes, TCD and King's Inns. Secretary of Dept. of External (Foreign) Affairs 1945; ambassador to Britain 1950. Ireland's first permanent representative to the UN 1956 and President of its General Assembly 1960. His presidency witnessed the famous shoe-banging incident involving USSR president Kruschev. Chancellor of Dublin Univ. (TCD) 1963.

BOYDELL, WILLIAM C. (1920). Maltster. An affable man who organised shooting parties for members. ALAN (1940) and D.K. BOYDELL (1947) were also Members.

BRADY, SIR FRANCIS WILLIAM, BART. (1857). Born Dublin 1824. His father, Sir Mazière Brady, 1st Baronet, was three times Lord Chancellor of Ireland. A lineal descendant of the Nicholas Brady who, with Nahum Tate, was responsible for the metrical version of The Psalms. Educ. in London, QC 1860; Deputy Lieutenant of the City of Dublin. A founder and vice-president of the Royal Irish Academy of Music and author of several works on music.

Francis William Brady

BRINDLEY, THOMAS P. 1906–1978 (1959). Born Dublin. Educated Clongowes. Succeeded his father who was founder and Chairman of Brindleys, the printers, in Eustace Street – a firm synonymous with *The Racing Calendar*. A great golfing enthusiast, Hon. Sec. and Chairman of the Leinster Branch before becoming Chairman of the GUI in 1965/66. He had the good fortune to win a Life Membership to the SGC in 1963 during one of the Fund Raising Sweepstakes which were popular at the time. Chairman in 1970/72, he resided at the Club up to his death in 1978.

BRINDLEY, TONY 1902–1977 (1932). Educ. Clongowes and Downside, only son of Charlie, 'Keeper of the Match Book' from 1911 to 1921 and grandson of Thomas who held the same post with the Turf Club, 1891–1911. Tony's great-grandfather, also Charlie, came to Ireland from Staffordshire in 1838 and is the central figure in the Ward Union Hunt engraving in the Club's hallway. (See p. 86). A stockbroker at 24 Anglesea Street for more than 50 years, Tony served as President and Secretary of the Stock Exchange Golfing Society and was also a member of Portmarnock, Hermitage and Lahinch. Played rugby with Bective Rangers and succeeded his great friend Eddie Mulhern (1943) as Hon. Treasurer of the Leinster Branch, 1943. Served on the committee of the IRFU, 1947–53 with Cahir Davitt (q.v.). A first cousin of TOM BRINDLEY (1959), father of BASIL (1965), chairman 1987–9 and organiser-in-chief of the sesquicentennial celebrations 1990.

BYRNE, WILLIAM H. 1884–1917 (1890). FRIA, founded a century-old practice of enduing quality with a long tradition of service to the Club. His son RALPH 1877–1946 (1916) FRIA, was architect to the Club in the first half of this century. (See p. 35). William H. Byrne's nephew SIMON A. LEONARD 1903–1976 (1927) carried on this high architectural tradition as does his son MARK W. (1976), contributor to this volume (pps. 110–117). ANTHONY serves on the SGC Committee.

CLARKE, COL. T.H.M. (1921). CMG, OBE, DSO, of Marley Grange, Rathfarnham (subsequently owned by Philip Love [q.v.]). Came from England with his son F.HAROLD (1921) to manage Leopardstown Race Course. (see p. 84)

COCHRANE, SIR ERNEST C. (1908). From Craughlough, Co. Cavan. Chairman of Cantrell & Cochrane, inventors of the soda-water syphon.

COX, ARTHUR C. 1891–1965 (1920). Played an important legal role in the establishment of the Irish Free State 1922. Associated with Henry Harrison (q.v.). Solicitor to the ESB (see T. McLaughlin) and many other important industries. Pre-eminent amongst contemporary lawyers, he was austere and scholarly rather than clubbable. Retired to become a Jesuit and died in a motor accident in Africa.

DARGAN, WILLIAM J. (1905). Physician to St Vincent's hospital, a grandnephew of WILLIAM DARGAN 1799–1862 the railway engineer and entrepreneur. (See p. 66)

DAVITT, CAHIR (1928). President of the High Court. Son of MICHAEL 1846–1906, founder of the Land League. Enjoyed relaxing at the Club with friends like Tony Brindley (q.v.) and Leo Flanagan and his own brother DR ROBERT E. (1944). See rugby, squash rackets and hunting coverage in this volume.

DILLON, JAMES. 1902–1986 (1944). Born Dublin. Educ. UCG and King's Inns, called to the bar 1931. Manager of family business in Ballaghadereen, Co. Roscommon. TD for West Donegal 1932–7 and for Monaghan 1937–69. Deputy leader of Fine Gael, resigning in 1942 after opposing the all-party neutrality policy. Minister for Agriculture 1948–51 as independent member of the coalition government. Rejoined Fine Gael 1953 and again Minister for Agriculture 1954–7. Leader of the party 1950, president 1960. Retired to the back benches 1965. Gentleman and old-style politician, his broad culture and great knowledge of world affairs combined with his outstanding kindness to make him the quintessential model for members of the Club for which he was Trustee. His brother MYLES (1946) was senior professor in the school of Celtic Studies at the Dublin Institute of Advanced Studies.

DODD, WILLIAM H. (1892). Judge, MP. Educ. QUB. See p. 72.

DONELAN, JOHN O'CONNOR (1899). LRCPSI, RMS, Grangegorman Mental Hospital. Father of JOSEPH (1919) and grandfather of DERMOT (1940).

William H. Dodd

DOYLE, THOMAS A. Died 1986 (1943). Judge. Hon. Sec. for many years and Trustee 1964–1985. Patron of Dublin Grand Opera Society and President of Phoenix Cricket Club, Old Belvedere RFC., Collegians Boat Club.

ENNIS, EDWARD HENRY. (1896). Educ. Belfast, joined the *Freeman's Journal* as leader-writer in 1883, subsequently studying law at King's Inns, Dublin. Called to the Irish Bar 1886. Assistant Under-Secretary for Ireland 1908; private secretary to the Lord Chancellor 1892. Identified with the erection of the statue to Thomas Moore ('The meeting of the waters') in Dublin. He died in 1908.

Edward Henry Ennis

ESMONDE. An ancient Catholic land-owning family from the Wexford area who espoused the Nationalist cause. When the sons of Henry Grattan MP, 1746–1820, died without issue the Esmondes adopted the name 'Grattan' and continued the long tradition of parliamentary service. SIR THOMAS H. GRATTAN ESMONDE 1862–1935 (1918) resigned from the Kildare Street Club on becoming Nationalist MP in 1885. The family connection was resumed in 1960. THOMAS L. ESMONDE (1899) and SIR JOHN L. ESMONDE, SC, (1938) were also SGC Members.

FITZGERALD, ALEXIS. (1943). Legal and philosophical advisor to the Fine Gael party.

FOTTRELL, JOHN EDWARD. 1820–1898 (1874). Of a well-known legal family, chairman of the Dublin Gas Co. and of Rathmines UDC. See portrait, p. 62. His brother SIR GEORGE (1894) KCB, Clerk of the Crown and Peace, was an active SGC committeeman.

GARDNER, SIR ROBERT. 1838–1920 (1887). Born Ballymoney, Co. Antrim. Practised as an accountant in Dublin from 1867, founding the firm of Craig, Gardner and Co. Married three times. JP for the County and City of Dublin; chairman of Pembroke Town Council. His son JOHN (1894) was also a chartered accountant.

GEARY, ROY C. (1952). Statistician and conversationalist. Invited many Members to join him as founders of the Economic & Social Society of Ireland.

Sir Robert Gardner (*Institute of Chartered Accountants of Ireland*)

GEOGHEGAN, THOMAS. 1875–1964. First independent professional auditor of SGC, 1917. Director of National Bank. (See p. 121).

GILL, WILLIAM J. (1946). Publisher and printer. Great-grandson of MICHAEL HENRY (1794–1879) master printer and publisher at the Dublin University Press, and son of the United Irishman. Father of MICHAEL (1964), Managing Director of Gill and Macmillan Ltd., publishers of this history.

GILLMAN, DANIEL F. (1920). Of the well-known Cork family, a skilful administrator and cricketer (see p. 119). Hon. Sec. His brother DONAL had placed his historical collection at the disposal of this history.

GOULDING, SIR LINGARD. 1883–1935. Born Dublin, educ. Eton and Oxford, Dir. of W. & H.M. Goulding Ltd., Governor of Bank of Ireland. Extensive sporting interests included international honours in polo, cricket, hunting, angling.

GWYNN, STEPHEN LUCIUS. 1864–1950. (1919). Born Co. Donegal, grandson of William Smith O'Brien. Nationalist MP for Galway 1906–1919. Served in France 1914–17, receiving Legion of Honour. Novelist, poet, travel writer and authority on 18th century Ireland. Father of Aubrey Gwynn SJ.

HARRINGTON, SIR STANLEY 1856–1919 (1918). Also of Cork Yacht club, industrialist, distiller and banker. Senator NUI.

HARRISON, HENRY 1867–1954. (1907). See p. 75.

HEALY, MAURICE F. 1887–1943. (1919). Born in Cork, his father was MP for Cork and his uncle Tim the first Governor General of the Irish Free Sate 1922–28. Became a barrister in 1910, member of King's Council 1931 and the Recorder of Coventry 1941. His book, *The Old Munster Circuit* (1939), a witty account of his legal experiences in Cork, has been several times reprinted.

HOGG, JONATHAN (1903). Quaker, wholesale merchant and director of the Bank of Ireland. Number 2 on the first list of Dublin telephone subscribers, 1882.

HORNE, SIR ANDREW JOHN. (1892). Born Co. Galway 1856, educated at Clongowes, Dublin and Vienna. Vice-President RCPI, Master of the National Lying-In Hospital, Clinical Resident, Mater Hospital, Dublin. Joyce wove Horne's name into Bloom's visit to Holles St. His sons CAPT. A.J. and FRANCIS J. were also Members.

KELLY, AMBROSE ALIAGA 1872–1953 (1900 Life) Hon. Sec. 1904–10. consul for the King of Spain. Sons CHRISTOPHER (1956) and CHARLES (1942) were Members.

KELLY, THOMAS ALIAGA. 1838–1916 (1875). Son of PATRICK and grandson of THOMAS LAPIN KELLY, both of whom are believed to have been Members from the earliest days. Successful wine merchants.

KELLY, THOMAS (1903) and EUGENE (1905) were wealthy New York cousins of Aliaga Kelly. They resided in great style when in Ireland.

LAVERY, CECIL. 1894–1967 (1924). Born Armagh, educ. UCD. Called to the bar 1915. Involved in Howth gun-running 1914 and stood by with Armagh division in the Rising of 1916. TD for North Co. Dublin 1935–8; attorney-general 1948 and elected to Seanad. Helped draft the Convention of Human Rights for the Council of Europe 1948 and the Republic of Ireland Bill 1949. Supreme Court judge 1950. A Steward of the Turf Club and active in the Arts Club. Brother of FRANK (1944).

LEONARD FAMILY. See BYRNE, WILLIAM H.

LOVE, PHILIP A. See p. 151.

LYNCH, SIR JOHN P. (1883 Life). Legal adviser to the Club in the first quarter of this century.

MACARDLE, SIR THOMAS C. (1916). DL. of Macardle Moore Brewery, Dundalk. Prominent businessman.

McDONNELL, SIR ALEXANDER. 1794–1875. PC. Chief clerk under THOMAS DRUMMOND (q.v.), Conservative Commissioner of Education. Widow gave donation to the building fund.

MacDONNELL, LORD (Anthony Patrick MacDonnell). 1844–1925. (1879). Of Palmfield, Co. Mayo. Educ. Queen's College, Galway. Entered Indian Civil Service and held several positions including Lieut.-Gov. of Bengal and of North West provinces before becoming Under-Sec. to Lord Lieut. of Ireland, 1902–1908.

Lord McDonnell

McDONNELL, RICHARD J. (1865). Died in 1929 as 'Father of the Club' leaving it a legacy of £200.

McLAUGHLIN, THOMAS A. 1896–1971. (1943). D. Eng., Executive with Siemens-Schuchert whom he persuaded to co-operate with Patrick McGilligan, Minister for Industry and Commerce, in the farsighted Shannon hydro-electric scheme.

MacMAHON, RT. HON. JAMES. 1865–1954. (1919). Secretary of the Post Office, Under-secretary at Dublin Castle 1918–22. Close friend of W.E. Wylie (q.v.) who wrote of him: 'His sanity and calm, his complete sincerity and his understanding of Irish problems had helped me time out of number'. His knowledgable administration contributed to the orderly withdrawal of the British from the Free State.

McVEAGH, TREVOR GEORGE. 1908–1968 (1959). Educated St. Columba's College and TCD. Solicitor, represented Ireland at hockey, tennis, squash and cricket (q.v.).

MALCOMSON, G.V. See p. 85.

MAHONY, DAVID B. (1933, Life). Civil servant. A most affable Hon. Sec. for many years.

MARTIN, CHARLES EDWARD, JP. 1839–1907. Born Dublin, educated Clongowes, senior of the firm of T. and C. Martin Ltd., North Wall. Governor and director of the Bank of Ireland, director of the Dublin Artisans' Dwelling Co., Commissioner of Irish Lights. His house in Donnybrook, Montrose, is now the headquarters of Radio Telefis Eireann (RTE). Matthew (Matt)

Talbot was a labourer at Martin's timberyard. Mother Mary Martin was a sister. Many relatives were SGC Members. CYRIL (1919), FRANK (1898) and THOMAS G. (1919) all served on the board of the Bank of Ireland.

MARTYN, GEORGE VALENTINE. c1870–1940. His family was from Curraghmore, Lough Corrib and he was an engineer on the Bombay-Baroda railway. Hon. Sec. during the troubled period 1916–22, service commemorated by the quaint print depicting clubmen at play in the Billiard Room. On retirement became an amateur historian, producing a monograph history of the Club in 1920. Resided at the SGC for the last 25 years of his life.

MEENAN, JAMES 1910–1987. (1941). Prof. of Economics UCD, barrister, journalist, economic historian. Chairman, Royal Dublin Society, Bank of Ireland and ESB (see GEARY, ROY). Combined great mental powers with activity in rowing, swimming and hill-walking. His wit, conviviality and scholarship will not readily be forgotten at the Club. Two brothers are Members.

Thomas Francis Molony

MOLONY, THOMAS FRANCIS, KC. (1897) Lord Chief Justice of Ireland. Born Dublin 1865, educ. TCD. Called to the Irish Bar 1887; QC 1899. Father of SIR HUGH (1955), engineer and Trustee.

MOORE, JOHN (1969), US Ambassador to Ireland 1969 to 1975. Followed his family tradition of dedicated political service to both countries. Together with his wife and daughter he lies buried in Deansgrange Cemetery. R.I.P. His younger brother RICHARD (1989) is now US Ambassador here. This traditional relationship with the American Embassy has been greatly appreciated at the Club.

MOORE, THOMAS LEVINS (1894). Brewer. He and his son ANDREW (1932), who d.1990, were prominent in horse-racing and hunting. In c1880 Thomas presented the Club with the engraving of the Ward Union Hunt. (See also MACARDLE).

MONAHAN, HENRY J. (1899 Life). QC. Hon. Sec. 1909–11. His father JAMES HENRY 1894–1878 MP, erstwhile counsel for Daniel O Connell, 1843–4, became an anti-Fenian judge.

MULLINS, MICHAEL BERNARD. SEE BIOGRAPHIES I

Sir James Murphy

MURPHY, SIR JAMES, BART., JP. (1907). Born Dublin 1843, member of the shipping firm of Palgrave, Murphy and Co. President of Dublin Chamber of Commerce 1902–4; Chairman of the Royal Bank of Ireland; Consul for the Imperial German Empire. His father MICHAEL (1887) and brother SIR MICHAEL were Members.

MYERSCOUGH, CYRIL (1944). Prominent in bloodstock and insurance circles. Conducted the Club's auction sweeps with great skill for many years. Member of the board of St Patrick's cathedral. Died 1985.

NIXON, SIR CHRISTOPHER JOHN, BART. (1880). Born Dublin 1849, educ. TCD and St Cecilia School of Medicine, Paris. Professor of Medicine at the Catholic University, Dublin; member of the Senate of the Royal University and first President of the Royal Veterinary College of Ireland.

NOLAN, R. ALAN. (1934). of Browne & Nolan, printers, produced the beautifully-marbled Club minute books. His aunt, Elizabeth Nolan, was mother of ARTHUR COX (q.v.).

NUGENT, SIR WALTER 1865–1955 (1901). Fourth Bart. Nationalist MP. Senator IFS, of the Turf Club and Bank of Ireland. (See SIR PERCY NUGENT portrait, p. 62).

Sir Christopher Nixon

O CALLAGHAN, T. FREDERICK. Served on the Committee in 1890s. Resided in the Club and died there in 1898 of an infectious disease.

O CONNELL, SIR JOHN ROBERT (1914). Solicitor, of Dublin and Cork, director of the National Bank, etc. Grandson of the Liberator. Retired to join the Jesuit order.

O CONOR DON. See p. 67.

O REILLY, BERTRAM (1918), Capt. CHARLES (1911) DSO and Major HERBERT J. (1910) were all of the John Power distillery family.

O MALLEY, DONOGH. 1921–68 (1966) Engineer and politician. Born Limerick, educ. UCG. Elected to the Dail for Limerick East 1954. Minister for Health 1965, for Education 1966. Introduced free post-primary education and proposed a controversial merger between UCD and TCD.

PIM. Quaker family of liberal outlook. Dissenters found other Dublin clubs uncongenial but were welcomed at the SGC. JONATHAN PIM (1905) was a judge and prominent public figure; H. LEOPOLD PIM (1886) a poplin manufacturer and Hon. Sec, SGC, 1902–4; JOSEPH TODHUNTER PIM (c1900) was a director of several companies including Pim Bros. of South Great George's St., the Bank of Ireland and transport undertakings.

PLUNKETT, SIR HORACE. 1854–1932. (1908) From 1899 took leading role in developing the co-operative movement, esp. among dairy farmers. Unionist MP for S. Co. Dublin 1892, first pres. of the Irish Agricultural Organisation Soc. 1894. His initiative led to the establishment of the Dept. of Agriculture and Technical Instruction, of which he became vice-president. Adopted Home Rule and campaigned 1914–22 for a united Ireland within the British Commonwealth. Senator 1922. His house at Kilteragh, Co. Dublin was burned during the Civil War, after which he moved to England.

PLUNKETT, THOMAS 1850–1927 (1878). DL. Barrister, of Portmarnock. Served as Trustee from 1906.

POWER, SIR JAMES TALBOT 1851–1916 (1871). Successful distiller and engineer. Entertained with great hospitality at Leopardstown Park and drove his coach and four greys with splendid panache. (See picture, p. 71) Trustee 1902–16. His brother SIR THOMAS 1863–1930 (1882)of Beaufield was the last baronet. Married Margaret, daughter of Thomas Martin (q.v.) but had no issue. His nephews, the Ryans and O'Reillys, succeeded him at the distillery (now Irish Distillers/Pernod Ricard). Sir Thomas was much praised for his unobtrusive work for the (R)IAC when they organised the Gordon Bennett race in 1903.

PURCELL, PIERCE (1927). Professor of Engineering, UCD. Became the 'grand old man' of Irish golf. Active in moving the university from Stephen's Green to Belfield. His son T. DESMOND (1943) was an international bridge player.

QUINLAN, HAROLD (1929) Studied medicine in Germany pre-1914 and became senior consultant at St Vincent's Hospital, then on the Green. Trustee until his death, 1978. His well-mannered dignity added greatly to the lunch table.

REDMOND, CAPT. WILLIAM ARCHER (1916) DSO. Barrister. Son of the politician JOHN E. MP. Sir Joseph M. Redmond (1905) of the Mater Hospital was not a relation.

SCROOPE, COL. CHARLES F. (1942). A gentle man who played tennis for Ireland. His family were strongly represented in the Club; DR GERVAISE W. (1913); ARTHUR (1917); HENRY (1919) and N.W. (1931).

Alfred. J. Smith
(see SMITH, Fred P.)

SMITH, DR FREDERICK P., DL (1926) Kevit Castle, Crossdoney, Co Cavan. Like his brother Professor Alfred, studied medicine in Germany. Although a Home Ruler represented Cavan at the Coronation of 1910, provoking indignation from northern Unionists. This political stance would not have been unusual in the Club at the time. His nephew Philip N. Smith (1922), solicitor in Cavan, frequently stayed at the Club. Three sons – DARAGH, LOUIS, AND NEIL – were also Members.

SMITHWICK, EDMOND. See Biographies I.

SOLOMONS, DR BETHEL. 1885–65 (1935). Educ. TCD, MRIA, etc. of the Rotunda Hospital and the Liberal Synagogue, prominent in bridge, rugby and hunting. Author of *One Doctor in his Time.*

SPRATT, GERALD (1948) and his cheerful son STANLEY (1942) were tobacco leaf importers. Gerald's daughter married Willoughby Hamilton (q.v.) whose son Hugh (1962) won the squash and snooker cups.

STOLBERG-STOLBERG, COUNT LEOPOLD (1861) KM, of Saxony and Readsland, Dunshaughlin. Married Mary Eddington of Dublin. See p. 72.

SUTTON, SIR ABRAHAM (1901). Of a Cork business family prominent in shipping, coal etc. His extremely conservative Catholicism was not unusual at the time. Succeeded Chief Baron Palles as President of Clongowes Union, 1920, as staunch Unionist and anti-Larkin. His nephew, ABRAM E. SUTTON (1917) was a Member, as is his grand-nephew RALPH SUTTON (1973) SC.

SWEETMAN, GERARD 1908–1970 Born Dublin, His mother Agnes was a daugher of Sir George Fottrell (q.v.). Educ. Beaumont and TCD. Solicitor. TD (Fine Gael) for Co. Kildare from 1948 until his death in a motor accident. Minister for Finance 1954–57 and advised the government to appoint T.K. Whitaker as head of the civil service and sec. of the Department. SWEETMAN, WALTER. Original Member, see p.63. Others of this prominent family would include EDMOND (1871); JOHN (1876); JAMES MICHAEL (1903), Prof.. of Law, UCD; ROGER MARY (1913) MP, BL.

Gerard Sweetman, TD

TAFT, WILLIAM HOWARD III (1953). US Ambassador to Ireland 1953–7. His welcome presence at the Members' table came as a breath of fresh air from the West after the stuffiness of 'The Emergency'.

TYNDALL, MAJOR DONALD A. (1946). Architect. Returned from prisoner of war camp in the East. Advised the SGC premises committee 1946 – and designed Guest Room.

WALDRON, LAURENCE AMBROSE. 1858–1923. Born Ballybrack, Co. Dublin. Member of Dublin Stock Exchange 1918. Chairman, Grand Canal Co; governor of the National Gallery and of Belvedere College. Nationalist MP for Stephen's Green Division of Dublin. *Bon vivant* and patron of the arts.

Queen's College, Cork
(*see* WINDLE)

WHELAN, LEO (1937). See p. 63.

WINDLE, SIR BERTRAM. 1858–1929. Scientist, author and President (1905–17) of Queen's College Cork. Member SGG 1906–21. Stayed at Club while attending Irish convention 1917/18 with Horace Plunkett (q.v.) and John Redmond. Hostilely received in QUC thereafter by Sinn Fein. Became Roman Catholic in 1883. Emigrated to University of Toronto where he died.

WOODS, SEAMUS D. (1943). Chief of Staff, IRA in Belfast 1920–22. Disgusted with politics after death of Michael Collins of whom he was a supporter. Became turf accountant and racehorse owner.

WYLIE, JAMES OWENS. 1845–*c*1920. Uncle of W.E. Wylie (q.v.). Born Rushvale, Co. Antrim. QC 1894. Judge of Supreme Court and Judicial Commissioner of the Irish Land Commission 1906. Unsuccessfully contested Mid-Armagh and North Tyrone as a Gladstone Liberal.

WYLIE, WILLIAM EVELYN. 1881–1964. Born Dublin, son of a Presbyterian minister. Educ. Coleraine and TCD, where he was an outstanding racing cyclist. SGC 1908. Served with the Officers' Training Corps, TCD, during the 1916 Rising and acted as prosecuting counsel at the courts martial of its

James Owen Wylie

leaders (See p. 80). High Court Judge 1920 and again, after the establishment of the Irish Free State, in 1924. Judicial Commissioner of the Irish Land Commission. Played a prominent role in Club affairs (see p. 114) in which he resided during his latter years. Chairman of the Executive Committee of the Royal Dublin Society, where he was largely responsible for establishing the international prestige of the Horse Show. Enthusiastic sportsman (p. 85) and former Master of the Ward Union Staghounds.

YEATS, WILLIAM BUTLER. 1865–1939. (1914). Poet, dramatist, founder of the Abbey Theatre, Senator, Nobel prizewinner and 'great gentleman'. (Donagh McDonagh).

Appendices

Appendix I

ORIGINAL MEMBERS 1840

Berwick, Walter		Trustee 1838 onwards
Blake, Hon. Anthony		Committee 1840–41
Brady, Sir. Maziere		Portrait
Clarke, Thomas		Committee 1840 onwards
Cogan, W.M.V.		Portrait
Cloncurry, Lord Edward (Lawless)		Committee 1837–40
Corballis, John Richard, *B.L.*		Committee 1837–40
Curran, Wm. Henry,	4th son of John Philpot	Committee 1840 onwards
Dickson, Sam		Committee 1837–40 &1843
Dunne, Jeremiah		Committee 1837–40 &1843
Fitzgerald, Peter Nugent.		Committee 1840
Fitz-simon, Christopher	Married Margaret O'Connell	Committee 1838 onwards
Graham, George		Committee 1840 onwards
Hudson, Rev. E.G.		Trustee 1838 onwards
Hudson, Henry. M.D.		Committee 1840 onwards
Hudson, William		Committee 1840 onwards
Johnston, Robert, B.L.	(not identified)	Committee 1839 onwards
Lyne, Cornelius, B.L.		Committee 1837 onwards
McCarthy, Alexander, B.L.	Cork	Committee 1836 onwards
MacDonald, Norman H.		Committee 1841
Mahony, Pierce K . M.P.	Bust	Committee 1841 onwards
Mullins, Michael Bernard		Club Architect
Nangle, John H.		Committee 1839–41
Nugent, Sir Percy		Committee 1839 onwards
O'Brien, Judge James		Portrait
O'Brian, Samuel, Solicitor		Honorary Secretary
O'Connell, Daniel	See Note "O'Connell's Brigade"	
O'Connell, Morgan		Committee 1840 onwards
O'Conor Don, Charles Owen, M.P.		
O'Conor Don, Denis M.P.		Founder member Reform Club, presumed S.G.C.
Pigot, David R.	Judge	Portrait
Roe, George M.D.		Committee 1838+1841–2
Rorke, Laurence, B.L.		Committee 1839+1841
Sadlier, John	Banker	Solicitor to Letter Patent,
Sausse, Matthew, B.L.	Chief Justice of Bombay	
		Committee 1841
Scully, Vincent, Q.C., M.P.		Committee 1839 onwards

Seagrave, Patrick, J.P.		Committee 1842
Smithwick, Edmond		
Sweetman, Walter B.L.		Trustee 1837 onwards
Symes, Thomas B.L.	(not identified)	Committee 1842
Tighe, Robert, B.L.		Committee 1837 onwards
Trench, Hon. Charles James B.L.		Committee 1839 onwards

Note (1)   Not complete list.
Note (2)   Union Club committeemen are not necessarily 'Original Members'

177

Appendix II

THE LETTERS PATENT

1. *Victoria by the Grace of God*
2. *of the United Kingdom of Great Britain and Ireland Queen,*
   Defender of the faith and so forth. To all unto whom these
3. *presents shall come, GREETING WHEREAS Edward Gustavus*
   Hudson, Walter Berwick and Walter Sweetman in their petition
   humbly represented unto
4. *our Lieutenant General and General Governor of that part of*
   our Kingdom of Great Britain and Ireland called Ireland that
   by indenture of lease having date the eleventh day
5. *of June one thousand eight hundred and thirty six Joseph Earl*
   of Milltown granted and demised unto William Shearman that
   dwelling house and premises known as number ten Stephen's
   Green North in the city of Dublin to hold for a term
6. *of ninety nine years at the yearly rent of one hundred and fifty*

*pounds sterling and said indenture contained a covenant on
the part of the said William Shearman That he and his assigns
should keep said house and premises insured during*

7. *the whole of said term in a sum of one thousand five hundred
    pounds at least and the said William Shearman accordingly
    purchased such policy of insurance in the month of September
    following That Petitioners with several*

8. *other gentlemen having formed themselves into a club called
    "The Union Club" entered into an arrangement with the said
    William Shearman for the purpose of using said house as a club
    house and same was accordingly used and known*

9. *by the name of the "Union Club House" up to the month of
    February last That the said William Shearman purchased
    an insurance on his own life with the Caledonian Insurance
    Office in the month of September one thousand eight hundred
    and thirty seven*

10. *for the sum of one thousand five hundred pounds and also
    purchased one other insurance with the same office whereby the
    Furniture and Fixtures of said house were insured against fire
    in the sum of five hundred pounds That the said William*

11. *Shearman in the month of October one thousand eight hundred
    and thirty seven borrowed from the Directors of said Insurance
    company a sum of one thousand two hundred pounds and to
    secure the repayment thereof with interest at six per cent*

12. *conveyed to said Directors said dwelling house and premises
    Furniture and said several Policies of Insurance by way of
    mortgage subject to redemption, That by deed of Partnership
    having date the twenty seventh day of April one*

13. *thousand eight hundred and thirty nine made between William
    Shearman Henry Rosenthal and Henry Barre De Ballicourt it
    was agreed between them that they should henceforth carry on
    said Club house and by deed of equal date the said*

14. *Shearman assigned to the said Rosenthal and De Ballicourt two
    undivided third parts or shares of his the said Shearman's Equity
    of Redemption in said dwelling house and premises Furniture
    and policies of insurance TO HOLD to the said*

15. *Rosenthal and De Ballincourt as tenants in common as therein
    That by indenture bearing date the third day of August one
    thousand eight hundred and thirty nine the said William
    Shearman assigned his remaining undivided third part or
    share of said premises to the said*

16. *Rosenthal and De Ballincourt and by deed of equal date said
    partnership of Shearman, Rosenthal and De Ballincourt was
    dissolved so far as the said Shearman was concerned, that all
    said several deeds have been duly registered in the public office for*

17   *Registering Deeds in the city of Dublin and said Messieurs Rosenthal and De Ballicourt carried on and keep said Club House and premises from such month of August to the month of February last when said Union Club was dissolved That a committee of*

18   *Gentlemen members of said Union Club having in the same month formed a resolution to purchase the said club house and premises from said Messieurs Rosenthal and De Ballicourt and Petitioners were deputed by said committee to enter into a*

19   *negotiation for such purpose which petitioners accordingly did and an arrangement for that purpose was entered into between Petitioners and said Rosenthal and De Ballicourt That by deed of assignment bearing date the sixteenth day of*

20   *March one thousand eight hundred and forty the said Henry Rosenthal and Henry Barre De Ballicourt for the consideration of one thousand three hundred pounds assigned and made over to petitioners the interest in the lease of said dwelling*

21   *house and premises furniture and said several policies of insurance subject to said mortgage debt of one thousand two hundred pounds and by virtue of such assignment Petitioners are now possessed thereof in trust for said club That*

22   *Petitioners have discovered that the said Messieurs Rosenthal and De Ballicourt are aliens and that although they have been resident in this country for several years they have not obtained letters of denization or in other respects performed*

23   *the acts required by the statutes in that respect made and provided That by reason of the said Messieurs Rosenthal and De Ballicourt being aliens Petitioners are advised that it is necessary for them to obtain a grant or confirmation from the*

24   *Crown of all said premises AND Petitioners showed that they made the purposes of a Club House and that except as members of said Club they have no further interest therein*

25   *AND Praying that our said Lieutenant General and General Governor of Ireland would take the matter of their petition into consideration and direct that the conveyance be made to Petitioners of said dwelling house and premises*

26   *furniture and policies of insurance by said Henry Rosenthal and Henry Barre De Ballicourt might be confirmed by grant thereof from the Crown as in such cases usual or for such other relief in the premises as to our said*

27   *Lord Lieutenant General and General Governor of Ireland should seem fit AND WHEREAS our said Lord Lieutenant General and General Governor of Ireland did refer the said petition with the declaration of Mr. John Sadlier Solicitor*

28   *for the Petitioners verifying the said petition as also the several*

documents therein referred to unto our Attorney General in Ireland aforesaid to consider the said petition and to report unto our said Lieutenant General and General

29 Governor of Ireland what might be proper to be done thereon and our said Attorney General being of opinion that our said Lieutenant General and General Governor of Ireland might if he should be pleased so to do recommend

30 Us to grant to the said Petitioners our Letters Patent granting the said dwelling house and premises in said Petition set forth to the said Edward Gustavus Hudson, Walter Berwick and Walter Sweetman upon trust for

31 the purposes in said petition mentioned AND WHEREAS our said Attorney General did in obedience to the order of our said Lieutenant General and General Governor of Ireland bearing date the twenty ninth Day of April one thousand eight

32 hundred and forty prepare the draft of a letter for our Royal Signature granting the prayer of the said Petitioners in accordance with the opinion of our said Attorney General we taking the premises into our Royal consideration have

33 been graciously pleased to grant unto the said petitioners our Royal letters patent for the purposes aforesaid Know ye therefore that we of our special grace certain knowledge and mere motion by and with the advice and

34 consent of our right trusty and entirely Beloved cousin and Counsellor Hugh Baron Fortesque commonly called Viscount Ebrington our Lieutenant General and General Government of that part of our said United Kingdom of

35 Great Britain and Ireland called Ireland and according to the tenor of our letters under our Privy seal and Royal sign manual bearing date of our court at Saint James's the twelfth day of May one thousand eight hundred

36 and forty in the third of our reign and now enrolled in the Rolls of our High Court of Chancery in Ireland aforesaid have given and grant AND by these presents We do give and grant for Us our heirs and successors We do

37 given and grant unto the said Edward Gustavus Hudson, Walter Berwick and Walter Sweetman the said dwelling house and premises in their said petition set forth upon trust for the purposes in the said petition mentioned AND FURTHER

38 of our like special grace and certain knowledge and mere motion by and with the advice and consent aforesaid We do give and grant that these our letters patent or the enrolment or exemplification thereof shall be in all things good sufficient valid and

39 effectual in the law according to the true intent and meaning

thereof without any further grant or confirmation to be from
us had procured or obtained PROVIDED always that these our
letters patent be enrolled in the Rolls of our

40 *high Court of Chancery in Ireland aforesaid within the space*
of six calender months next ensuing the date of these presents
In witness whereof we have caused these our letters to be made
Patent Witness Hugh Baron Fortesque

41 *our Lieutenant General and General Governor of Ireland at*
Dublin the twenty second day of July in the fourth year of our
reign.

Three rolls	3	14	10
Clerk inspecting stamps		1	0
	3	15	10

entered and examined by G Hatchell, Clerk of Inrolments
Christopher Fitzsimons
Clerk of the Crown
and Hanaper

Inrolled in the Rolls of her
Majesty's High court of
Chancery in Ireland the
twenty eight day of July
one thousand eight hundred
and forty.
Francis J. Nash
Temporary Officer under
6 George 4 cap 20

WHY THESE LETTERS PATENT?

In 1840 the legal vehicles available to the promoters of any enterprise were limited to three:-

(i)	a Common Law Company
(ii)	a special Act of Parliament Corporation
(iii)	a Royal Charter (Letter Patent) Corporation

(i) A Common Law Company was merely a large partnership without corporate existence or limitation of liability.

It was the practical usage – and abuses – of this 'illegitimate' combination which gave rise to the Companies Acts from 1844 onwards. This modernised procedure was not much used in Ireland until the first great Companies Consolidation Act of 1862.

(ii) A special Act of Parliament could confer rights on corporations.

The Anonymous Partnership Act 1781 and the Canal Companies Acts were examples of up-to-date practical type of commercial legislation passed by our Parliament until 1800.

The Dublin and Kingstown Railway Company Act 1831, approved by William 1V, was a contemporary example.

(iii) Royal Charter/Letters Patent – this was a prerogative of the Crown under Common Law since Magna Carta times.

The Royal Charter procedure was sparingly used because it was ponderous and costly. The Cork Butter Market 1823 was a contemporary example.

The 'Royal Sign Manual' on the 'Letters Patent' from Queen Victoria was an analogous, but more limited, Grant.

Aliens, such as Rosenthal and De Ballicourt, were prohibited from acquiring freehold or leasehold property. Any property acquired by them would, after the holding of an inquest of office, become Crown property. Consequently anyone who held property by lease or grant from an alien risked losing his title to it. To get around this it was necessary for the lessee or grantee to petition the Crown, in order that the Crown would, by issuing Letters Patent, forego its interest in the property and confirm the grant or lease made by the alien.

This document, therefore, represents a technical device to secure the Club's interest in the original lease of No.10 Stephen's Green by the Earl of Milltown.

It is a title to property and may not necessarily involve any Royal recognition or approval of the Club, or empower the Club or the trustees to perform any acts relating the business of the Club.

In this case therefore, while the Letters Patent narrated the power of the Trustees to conduct a club, its primary function must have been to cure the defect in title. However, in the political climate of the time the Liberal Viceroy H.E. Viscount Ebrington would undoubtedly have supported benevolently the plans of O'Connell's followers.

The 'special grace' and favour of the Crown did forego a punitive right to sequestrate the Club's property.

ADVANTAGES OF THE LETTERS PATENT

(i) Clarified title as successors to the Union Club, Q.V.
(ii) Conferred prestige on this new Club for Liberal Reformers in Ireland. It proclaimed to the world at large that the Club had Royal 'special grace' and favour.
(iii) Empowered the Club to use its exclusive Common Seal.

The Letters Patent of 1840 has no longer any practical significance in defining the Club's legal title or powers.

I do not know how frequently these Letters Patent were petitioned in Ireland at the time, or how much it all cost the Club.

The Personages mentioned in the Letters Patent have mostly been described elsewhere:-

Name	Function	Reference
Ballicourt, Henry De Barre	An alien Financier	No information traced
Berwick, Walter	Trustee	Biography
Ebrington, Viscount	Viceroy	'The Castle'
Fitzsimon, Christopher	Clerk of the Crown	Biography
Holbrook	Engraver	Biography
Hudson, Rev. Edward	Trustee	Biography
La Touche	Former Owners	Bankers-Chapter
Millotwn, Joseph, Earl of	Landlord	Biography
Rosenthal, Henry	An alien Financier	Tobacconist
Sadlier, John	Solicitor	Banker-Chapter
Shearman, William	Tenant Manager of 'The Union Club'	
Sweetman, Walter	Trustee	Biography

The Tenant Proprietors of no. 10 (now 9) Stephen's Green in 1836–1839 were shadowy figures:-

William Shearman (sic) is described in the Directory as the 'proprietor of the Union Club'. He then vanished.

Henry Rosenthal presumably was the Tobacconist trading at No. 38 Nassau Street. He was an alien.

Baron De Ballicourt – an alien, apparently resident in Dublin but not identified.

Directories show occupiers of the property:-

1831–36	–	Robert La Touche, Banker (retired Colonel, M.P.) of Harristown, Co. Kildare. He was son of John who died 1805, and nephew of Peter, of Bellevue, died 1828. See 'Bankers', p. 51.
1837	–	'---Sharpe' (sic)
1837	–	William Shearman (sic), Proprietor of Union Club.
1839–40	–	Union Club.
1840	–	Stephen's Green Club.

Appendix III

Committee Membership Structure 1837–1843

UNION CLUB 1837/40		STEPHENS GREEN CLUB ONLY 1840 ONWARDS	
COMMITTEE WHO SERVED BOTH UNION AND S.G.C.		SGC Committee-men 1840 onwards (not ex-Union)	
Berwick, Walter	1838 onwards	**Blake, Hon. Anthony**	1840/41
Cloncurry, Lord Edward (Lawless)	1837/1840	**Clarke, Thos.**	1840 onwards
Corballis, John R. B.L.	1837/1840	**Curran, Wm. H.**	1840 onwards
Dickson, Sam	1939/40 + 1843	Fitzgerald, Peter N.	1840
Dunne, Jeremiah	1839/40 + 1843	**Grehan, George**	1840 onwards
Fitzsimon, Christopher	1833 onwards	**Hudson, Henry MD**	1840 onwards
Hudson, Rev. E.G.	1838 onwards	**Hudson, William**	1840 onwards
Johnston, Robert B.L.	1839 onwards	**Mahoney, Pierce K. MP**	1841 onwards
Lyne, Cornelius B.L.	1837 till death	**MacDonald Norman H.**	1841
McCarthy, Alexander B.L.	1838 onwards	**O'Connell, Morgan MP**	1840 onwards
Nangle, John H.	1839/1841	**O'Ferrall, Jas, BL**	1840
Nugent, Sir Percy	1839 onwards	**Sausse, Mathew BL**	1844 onwards
Roe, George M.D.	1838 + 1841/2	**Seagrave, Pat. J.P.**	1842
Rorke, Laurence B.L.	1839 + 1841	**Symes, Thos.**	1842
Scully, Vincent QC., MP.	1839 onwards		
Sweetman, Walter B.L.	1837 onwards		
Tighe, Robert B.L.	1837 onwards		
Trench, Hon. CJ. B.L.	1839 onwards		

VICEREGAL HOUSEHOLD – on Founding Committee, Union Club.

Barron, Capt, John W. ADC (h.p.)	1837
Bernal, Ralph Capt ADC	1837
Burke, Thomas J ADC	1837/8
Connellan, Cory, BL Gentleman at Large	1837/38
Fitzroy, Henry Gentleman at Large	1837
Hankey, Major 8th Hussars	1837/8
Higgins, Capt	1837/8
Quill, Lt. Col	1837/39
Sheridan, F.C. Gent. of Bedchamber	1837/8
Synge, Colonel	1837/8
Vaughan, Hon G. Master of Horse	1837

OTHER UNION COMMITTEE-MEN (Not
    S.G.C. Committee)

Brown, Capt Arthur	1839	
Darley, Henry B.	1837/9 Biog.	
Fingall, Earl of	1838/9	
Fitzpatrick, J. Wilson. MP	1837 Biog.	
Goold, George	1839/40	
Holmes, John, Galway	1839	
Howley, John QC.	1837/9 Biog.	
Mullins, Thomas B.L.	1838 Biog.	
Plunket, Hon. Patrick	1837/8 Biog.	
Sausse, Mathew B.L.	1839	Elected SGC. Jan. 1844 and Jan. 1845

UNION CLUB SECRETARY,   SGC SECRETARY

Byrne, Michael Esq   **O'Brien, Samuel M. Esq**
                                          14 Holles St. Elected May 1840

Appendix IV

Daniel O'Connell and the Masonic Order

GRAND LODGE OF A.F. & A. MASONS OF IRELAND
Grand Secretary's Office,
Freemasons' Hall,
17, Molesworth Street,
Dublin 2.

Mr. Cornelius Smith,   *31st August, 1987.*
Modeshill,
34 Stillorgan Grove,
Blackrock,
Co. Dublin.

Dear Mr. Smith.

Thank you for your enquiry regarding Daniel O'Connell and his membership of the Masonic Order. The Grand Lodge of Freemasons of Ireland was formed in 1725 and as such it is the second oldest Grand Lodge of Freemasons in the world. The earliest Grand Lodge is that of England, formed in 1717. The Grand Lodge is merely the governing body of all the subordinate lodges. The earliest datable Irish Masonic lodge is a Dublin one which was in existence in 1688. Others claim a similar antiquity, but there is no documentary evidence to support their claims.

The Grand Lodge building in Molesworth Street was erected in 1865 as the permanent home of the Dublin lodges and as the headquarters of the Order.

Daniel O'Connell joined Lodge No. 198 in Dublin in 1799, not an unusual thing for a man of his standing to do. At this time the Order's membership was predominently Catholic. O'Connell resigned from the Order in a rather public manner in 1837.

His membership and the general history of the Order in Dublin will be the subject of a public exhibition in our Museum next year.

Yours sincerely,

C.G. HORTON
Archivist

Note:
Since 1738 Papal Bulls had regularly been issued condemning the secret oath required by the Freemasons. Pope Gregory XVI had repeated this prohibition in 1832 which may have raised the issue. Daniel O'Connell retired from the Order but in 1837 his political enemies circulated a rumour that he was still a member. O'Connell then published a letter confirming that he had retired many years previously but that he believed the Freemasons had no evil tendencies in Ireland.

Did the Vatican have some premonition of the dangers of the P–2 Masonic Lodge and its own expensive link with the Banco Ambrosiano? – CFS.

Appendix V

LIST OF RECIPROCAL CLUBS

NORTHERN IRELAND

Armagh Club
Armagh

Tyrone Club
Omagh

Ulster Reform Club
Belfast

GREAT BRITAIN

Army and Navy Club
London

East India Sports and Public Schools Club
London

The Leeds Club
Leeds

Travellers' Club
London

United Oxford and Cambridge
London

University Club
Aberdeen

UNITED STATES OF AMERICA

Algonquin Club
Boston

The Army and Navy Club
Washington D.C

Chicago Athletic Association
Chicago

Detroit Athletic Club
Detroit

The Family
San Francisco

The New York Athletic Club
New York

Pittsburg Athletic Association
Pittsburgh

The University Club
Pittsburgh

The University Club of St. Louis
Saint Louis

CANADA

The Edmonton Club
Edmonton

Manitoba Club
Winnipeg

University Club of Vancouver
Vancouver, B.C.

AUSTRALIA

The Athenaneum Club
Melbourne

The Kelvin Club Limited
Melbourne

The Naval and Military Club
Melbourne

Newcastle Club
Newcastle

Tattersall's Club
Brisbane

OTHER COUNTRIES

Doha Club
Doha
Quatar

The Hong Kong Club
Central Hong Kong.

Seoul Club
Seoul, Korea

CHRONOLOGY

*A Club that is ignorant of its past
must surely be uncertain as to its future*

YEAR	STEPHEN'S GREEN CLUB	OTHER CLUBS for gentlemen	GENERAL HISTORY
13th Century	'The city's common pasture called the Green Acres of St. Stephen'.	King John's Charter for Dublin	Crusades. Black Death
c 1610	St. Stephen's Church on Speed's Map of Dublin	Friendly Brothers formed.	Cromwell in Ireland 1649
1660s	St. Stephen's Green laid out with gallows at Harcourt Street and Merrion Row. Lot 28 (No. 9) drawn by Waterhouse – sold on to Leeson [Milltown]	Rules of Billiards printed	Great Fire of London. Louis XIV King 1643/1715
1730s	No. 9 St. Stephen's Green built for Harman family circa 1730. Brooking's 'Prospect' 1728.	Freemasons of Dublin 'Hellfire Club' c. 1735.	Penal Laws. 'South Sea Bubble' bursts.
1750s	Lafrancini Brothers' stucco & staircase c. 1756. Rev. Cutts Harman at No. 9 from 1757 to 1784.	Turf club at Curragh. 1750. Dining club of Down Hunt, 1751. Friendly Brothers move to Dublin.	(R). D.S. formed 1731. Concessions to Catholics.
1760s	Robert Harman bequeaths No. 9 to brother Rev. Cutts, 1765.	Daly's Gambling Club opened 1763.	Spinning machinery revolutionised.
1770s	Ann Parsons (Née Harman) died 1775.	Ely House (now "Knights" Clubhouse) built.	Daniel O'Connell born 1775. American Declaration of Independence 1776.
1780s	Lawrence Parsons, Earl of Rosse, inherits No. 9 in 1784.	Kildare Street Club founded 1782.	Grattan's Parliament Bank of Ireland formed 1783.
1790s	Malton's etching of Green published 1796.	Law Club formed 1791/1899. Sackville St. Club formed 1794/1923.	Battle of Boyne 1792. 'Year of Liberty' 1798. French Revolution.

YEAR	STEPHEN'S GREEN CLUB	OTHER CLUBS FOR GENTLEMEN	GENERAL HISTORY
1800	Great houses for sale.	Gentry commence move to London.	Act of Union.
c 1812	No. 9 passes from Rosse to Peter La Touche who died 1828. No. 9 becomes a boarding house.	Limerick Club formed 1813.	Napoleon invades Russia U.S.A. at war with Great Britain.
1815	St. Stephen's Green railed in for key holders 1815/1876.	Friendly Brothers in Sackville St. 1820.	O'Connell kills D'Esterre in Duel. Waterloo.
1825	Walter Scott visits son, Capt. Walter, at No. 9.	Gas lighting for Billiard Rooms at Limerick Club.	Babbage calculating machine. Goya, Constable and Turner.
1829	O'Connell "The Liberator"		Catholic Emancipation.
1832		HUSC formed by Army.	Dublin and Kingstown. Railway 1834.
1836	Lease No. 9 – 99 years from from Milltown to Sharman	Reform Club on Pall Mall.	Liberals and O'Connell in power.
1837	Union club formed at No. 9 with Sharman as manager	Celibacy for TCD Fellows abolished	Victoria Queen 1837/1901. RIC formed
1840	Stephen's Green Club takes over by Letters Patent		Repeal Association founded by O'Connell.
1841/5	No. 9 altered and extended. M.B. Mullins Architect	Soyer, Chef at Reform Club.	Chartists not supported by O'Connell. Potatoe blight – Famine until 1849.
1847	Stephen's Green Club offers hospitality to HUSC	HUSC move to No. 8 St. Stephen's Green.	European Rebellions O'Connell dies 1847
1849		University Club formed from TCD	Queen Victoria's successful visit to Dublin. Cholera epidemic.
1850s	Drainage improvements for St. Stephen's Green. Members active in formation of National Gallery.	University Club at No. 17 St. Stephen's Green.	Cardinal Newman at No. 86 St. Stephen's Green. I.R.B. + Fenians formed. Sadlier Bank collapse 1856.
1860s	Stephen's Green Club offers hospitality to Kildare Street Club.	Kildare St. Club burned down. Freemasons at Molesworth Street.	American Civil War.

191

YEAR	STEPHEN'S GREEN CLUB	OTHER CLUBS FOR GENTLEMEN	GENERAL HISTORY
1870s	St. Stephen's Green presented by Lord Ardilaun. Stephen's Green Club added bedrooms and porte cochère. Esmonde (Home rule M.P.) resigns Kildare St. Club.	City of Dublin Working Man's Club. HUSC bay windows 1878	Gladstone disestablished Church of Ireland and supports Home Rule.
1880s	Staff forbidden to wear moustaches. Telephone installed 1884	Catholic Commercial Club 1882/1973. Ulster Reform Club founded for Liberals 1880. Ulster Reform Club anti-Home Rule 1886. Friendly Brothers at 22 St. Stephen's Green.	Land War. Parnell & Davitt. I.R.F.U. 1880. Institute of Chartered Accountants 1888. Benz motoring in Manheim.
1890s	Lawrence photo of St. Stephen's Green 1895 Electricity ousts gas lighting. Shed for members' bicycles.	Cork Club card case. HUSC admits civilians.	Wyndham Acts and Land War. First Rugby Triple Crown 1894.
1901/5	Mansard bedrooms added Stephen's Green Club. Porte cochère enclosed Debentures £3,200 @ 5% (Redeemed by 1973) Lease renewed 500 years @ £200 p.a.	(R).I.A.C. formed All clubs decorated for Queen Victoria's visit. 1900.	Boer War brings prosperity to Ireland. James Joyce leaves 'St. Stephen's my Green' for Paris. Parnellite split. Redmond, M.P. leader.
1907/8	Membership List printed with new Bye-laws 1906 Telephone Account fixed at £10 per annum.	United Arts Club formed. Ed. Martyn wins case v. Kildare Street Club.	'Fusiliers' Arch. National University Boss Croker's *Orby* wins Epsom Derby.
1911	Additional accommodation and squash court.	Clubs decorated for George V visit.	Germany confronts France at Agadir. Strikes in Britain.
1913	Strike held up repairs – Bar and Toilets		Larkin v. W.M. Murphy. Great Strike
1914/18	'Roll of Honour', many members serving. "Easter 1916" written by W. B. Yeats. Auditor appointed 1917.	HUSC occupied by British Army 1916.	Ulster Divisions sacrificed at the Somme 1916.
1922/3	Punchestown Hut purchased from Sackville St. Club – £150 SGC staff did not join strike	HUSC suffers loss of members. Kildare St. and HUSC	Departure H.M. Forces from I.F.S. Civil War and Strikes

YEAR	STEPHEN'S GREEN CLUB	OTHER CLUBS FOR GENTLEMEN	GENERAL HISTORY
1922/3		occupied by "Irregulars" Sackville Street closes – mostly to Kildare Street Club.	
1924/5	Membership List printed with new Bye-laws Lady guests admitted.	HUSC/Stephen's Green merger rejected	Shannon Scheme (Thos. McLoughlin)
1928	Second billiard room closed. New Bar.	Joint club meetings about Licencing Laws.	Mussolini and Nazis emerge.
1929	'Reading Out' dinner abolished.		Wall Street Crash. Great depression.
1930s	Stephen's Green Club closed for major repairs.	Leinster Club closed down. 1936.	DeValera, Economic War.
1940s	Centenary Dinner Subscription held @ £5	Clubs cope with shortages of food, drink & fuel.	'The Emergency' 1939/1945.
1950s	Financial stringency inhibits repairs. Orpen artwork presented.1954 Wylie snooker cup 1956	HUSC subscription raised to fifteen guineas, 1952 (Same as SGC)	Programme for Economic Expansion 1958.
1960s	Liberalised admission of guests & ladies to Club House.	Lady Associates at HUSC. 1964	Civil Rights March to Derry 1969.
1970s	5% Debentures all redeemed by 1973.	Kildare Street/University Clubs merge 1976.	Ireland in E.E.C. 1974. Opec Oil crises.
1980s	Financial problems overcome Relocation debate resolved. Major repairs & renovations 1983/90	Expansion of Club reciprocal arrangements internationally.	Anglo Irish Agreement at Hillsborough 1985.
1990s	Sesquicentennial celebrations – racing, music, ball, luncheon attended by H. E. Dr. Patrick J. Hillery.		Liberalisation in Eastern Europe and South Africa.

Index

198